JUPITER MOON COOK BOOK

JANET BUCKINGHAM

LIVE WIRE BOOKS

D1211942

First published in 2004 for Hopper Island Holdings by

Live Wire Books,
The Orchard, School Lane,
Warmington, Banbury,
Oxon. OX17 1DE
Tel: 01295 690624

E-mail: livewirebooks@aol.com

The right of Janet Buckingham to be identified as the author of this work has been asserted in accordance with the Copyright, Designs and Patents Act 1988.

ISBN 0-9542860-4-9

A catalogue record for this book is available from the British Library.

Photographs by Claude Tilche

Designed by Dick Malt
Printed in Great Britain by Witley Press,
Hunstanton, Norfolk

For 'Le Capitaine' JT, and his soul mate RBT

Contents

Acknowledgements

I would like to thank the following:

Claude Tilche: a special thanks for his wonderful photography. Joanne O'Neill, who typed endless recipes and helped me overcome the idiosyncrasies of the computer. Anita d'Oulhaye, Marie-Christine Poggesi, Dinah Voisin and Maite Manjón who translated the fish dictionary. Professor Hardy Long Frank for her help in editing the book for the U.S.A. With fond memories of Jean Trabant and some of her delicious recipes. Corinna Seidat for the photograph of *Jupiter Moon* and Anne Francis for her support and help.

A huge thanks to my partner, John Tully and son Rohan who have tried and tested all the recipes over the years. And to my mother, Joan Buckingham, who taught me to appreciate good food. Thanks too, to my family and friends, sailors and landlubbers alike, who have supported the idea of publishing this book.

Last, but not least, the publishers, Michael and Jill Cable of Live Wire Books who have made it a reality.

The Author is pleased to make a donation from the proceeds of the sales of this book to the Royal National Lifeboat Institution.
(Registered Charity Number 209603).

Dog Bowls

As someone whose previous sailing experience had been limited to a trip across our local reservoir in a small dinghy, I was more than a little apprehensive when my wife took it upon herself to volunteer me as a crew member aboard her brother's 65ft yacht for the 2,700-mile trans-Atlantic ARC race. She thought it would be a rather jolly way to mark my 60th birthday! To compound the felony, she then nominated me as the ship's cook to make up for the fact that as far as the actual sailing was concerned, I most certainly didn't know the ropes.

Fortunately, the rest of the crew turned out to be dedicated racers rather than pleasure cruisers – so hungry for victory that they were quite happy for mealtimes to be more like pit stops, the preferred style of dining being neatly summed up as 'dog bowl'.

'You need to knock up the sort of stuff that can be dished up in one of these,' explained the skipper at the pre-race briefing, reaching into a cupboard and producing a nest of plastic bowls of the sort that are normally to be found in a corner of the kitchen floor with the name Fido written on the side.

I must have got it vaguely right because we duly won the event, coming in only a few hours outside the previous record for the crossing, and there was never a hint of mutiny over the endless rotation of chilli con carne, spaghetti Bolognese and chicken curry.

But, as a virgin sailor – and cook – I have to admit that despite no less than 14 'crashes' and the total and spectacular disintegration of our entire steering mechanism in a Force Seven gale and heavy seas in mid-Atlantic, the most frightening part of the whole venture as far as I was concerned was standing in the middle of the supermarket in Gran Canaria trying to work out what quantities and what sort of provisions would be needed to keep a crew of nine well-fed for anything between twelve and eighteen days. I ended up with a dozen well-stacked trolleys – and my fingers firmly crossed.

How much simpler and less stressful it would have been for me if only I had been armed with Janet Buckingham's excellent *Jupiter Moon Cookbook*.

And how much tastier for my crew of salty old seadogs! They might even have been persuaded to throw away their dog bowls and break out the best plastic plates.

Named after the boat owned by Janet and her partner John Tully, and benefiting from her many years of first-hand experience, this very practical and easily navigable book not only features a varied selection of delicious and imaginative recipes, but it is also packed with invaluable tips about the planning of menus, the selection, purchase and storage of provisions for voyages of varying durations and all the most vital do's and don't's of life in the galley.

I wouldn't dream of setting sail again without a copy tucked into my kitbag or safely stowed aboard.

Michael Cable
Publisher
Live Wire Books

Introduction

It was some years ago, while preparing to deliver our newly acquired yacht *Jupiter Moon* from the cold, damp shores of the River Hamble in the UK to the sun-soaked Mediterranean, that I first recognised the need for a comprehensive sailing cookery book, a handy, compact volume with imaginative but uncomplicated recipes that would be easy to prepare in the confined space of a small galley without involving too many pots and pans. What I really wanted was the sort of manual that would provide inspiration as well as guidance, helping me to produce delicious, mouth-watering meals to cheer up a cold, tired and dispirited crew or to celebrate the end of a great day's sailing.

Earlier voyages on our previous boat *TaiPan* had been limited to crossings within the Mediterranean, where trips to Corsica, Italy, Spain and Sardinia were usually completed within 48 hours. The 15 years we spent sailing in the Mediterranean had taught me the special requirements for cooking afloat. As I discovered how to create tasty and exciting dishes that were easy to prepare, I was also sowing the seeds that have grown over time into the *Jupiter Moon Cookbook*.

It came as no surprise to our friends and relatives when we decided that we would like to venture towards more distant horizons and so we embarked on our first trans-Atlantic voyage to the Caribbean. During the 16 days it took us to sail from the Canaries to the West Indies, many more recipes were remembered, invented and improvised.

Some of the recipes in the *Jupiter Moon Cookbook* are old favourites such as Moules Marinieres. Others are ones that I have discovered myself such as Duck Breasts with Cranberries and Balsamic Vinegar, or Chicken Roasted with Tarragon and Lemon.

A large number of pasta dishes have been included for the very practical reason that pasta is such a wonderfully versatile ingredient – the dried variety, which lasts for many months, being especially useful at sea. With my partner John Tully and our son Rohan, I've spent some of my happiest days cruising the Mediterranean and the Caribbean, so you will find plenty of recipes inspired by the distinctive local cuisines of Provence, Italy and Spain, as well as a few from the West Indies.

Even when provisioning for longer trips, I always try to use fresh fruit, vegetables and herbs. And I always cook with olive oil. There is nothing quite like it for conjuring up the special flavours of the Mediterranean, in particular. Even so, as much as I love to cook with fresh ingredients, there are times when I see no harm in cheating a little. This is where the store locker recipes – scattered throughout the book and clearly marked – come into their own.

There is also a short section on barbecue cooking. If you've never tasted fresh tuna grilled on a barbecue off the stern of your boat, then you are missing out on one of life's greatest culinary delights. So, if you are going to be sailing in a warm climate then do invest in a barbecue. It's a tremendous boon for the cook, enables you to escape from the heat in the galley, and opens up a whole new range of possibilities. The results, so simple to achieve, are guaranteed to delight even the most jaded palate.

To make life easier on board I've listed essential kitchen equipment. There is also a suggested shopping list for the food locker, fridge and freezer, along with tips on how to package and store your food efficiently and safely.

Menu planning for a long journey can be a daunting task. To give you some ideas, I've included menu plans for both a short four-day sail and an extended sixteen-day voyage. The latter should prove extremely helpful for anyone planning a maiden trans-Atlantic voyage.

Finally, there is a section on Special Occasions – after all, you may find yourself celebrating Christmas Day, a birthday or Thanksgiving in mid-ocean. Many of the recipes in the book can be used if you are entertaining on board, something that is very much a part of boating life. To my mind, there is nothing more enjoyable than a long, leisurely meal afloat, shared with interesting companions and accompanied by lively discussions that can reach far into a moonlit night. Such occasions are among the true joys of life afloat.

Janet Buckingham 2004

Conversion Tables

All the recipes in this book list United Kingdom measures – both imperial and metric. America and United Kingdom solid weights are the same but the liquid quantities are different. American readers will be able to convert the UK liquid measurements in the recipes into US quantities by consulting the charts below. Australia is now using the metric system.

United Kingdom

lbs/oz	=	kg/gm
1 oz		28 gm
2		57
3		85
4		114
6		170
8		227
1 lb		454
2		907

fluid oz	=	tbsp	=	ml
$1/2$ fl oz		1 tbsp		15 ml
1		2		30
2		4		60
3		5		90
4		8		120
5		11		140
6		12		180
8		16		240

1 teacup	5 fl oz	140 ml
1 breakfast cup	10 fl oz	300 ml
$1/4$ UK imperial pint	5 fl oz	140 ml
1 UK imperial pint	20 fl oz	600 ml
$1^{3}/4$ UK imperial pint	35 fl oz	1 litre

1 tablespoon flour	$1/2$ oz/15g
1 tablespoon fat	$1/2$ oz/15g
1 tablespoon sugar	$1/2$ oz/15g

United States of America

1/3 cup	100 ml	3 1/2 UK fl.oz
1/2 cup (1 US gill)	115	4
2/3 cup (1/4 US pint)	140	5
1 cup	236	8
1 1/4 cups (1/2 US pint)	285	10
2 cups (1 US pint)	425	16
2 1/2 cups	570	20
4 cups (1 US quart)	1 litre	32
1 US tablespoon	20 ml	3/4

1 tablespoon breadcrumbs	1/2 oz	15 g
1 tablespoon cornstarch	1	25
1 tablespoon fat	1/2	15
1 tablespoon flour	1/2	15
1 tablespoon sugar	1	25
1 cup breadcrumbs	4	100
1 cup fat	8	225
1 cup flour	4	100
1 cup sugar	8	225
1 cup syrup/honey	12	350

Australia

1/4 teaspoon	1.25 ml
1/2	1.5
1	5
1 tablespoon	20
1/4 cup	62.5
1/3	83
1/2	125
1	250

Oven Temperatures and Gas Marks

Celsius	Fahrenheit	Gas Mark	Heat
110°C	225°F	$1/4$	Very Cool
120	250	$1/2$	Very Cool
140	275	1	Cool
150	300	2	Cool
160	325	3	Moderate
180	350	4	Moderate
190	375	5	Fairly Hot
200	400	6	Fairly Hot
220	425	7	Hot
230	450	8	Very Hot
240	475	9	Very Hot

Facing page: Maria's fruit & vegetable store - Mahon Market, Menorca.

PROVISIONING
AND ESSENTIAL STORES

Provisioning your boat, not only with the right items for you, but also with the right amount of each, is a daunting task - yet it is something that every galley cook gets better at with a little experience. Start by keeping a master list of staples that you always want on board. When you use an item on the list, cross it off so you remember to replace it next time you shop.

In planning menus, it helps if you know the next port of call and are familiar with its markets and supermarkets. But it is a rare wind that blows one into the port of destination on time. It is therefore essential to plan your menus in advance, whether for a day, weekend or longer. Take into account emergency meals and stores in case you arrive after the shops are closed - or, in the worst situation, you arrive several days later than planned.

Before leaving for a long trip, keep a note of what you normally eat at home, the chances are you won't drastically change your eating habits at sea. Then, as a rule of thumb, estimate how long your longest passage will be and add an additional 20 per cent.

Provisioning also applies to allowing for ample supplies of paper towels, toilet paper, soap etc. Friends of ours once ran short of fuel while crossing the Atlantic. They'd been stuck in the doldrums for several days while trying to make their way to St. Lucia. Eventually another boat came by, they chatted and discovered the crew were short of toilet paper. An exchange was made, toilet paper for diesel and both boats then departed happily on their way.

Learn to be versatile if you are missing an ingredient - don't be afraid to substitute with another. And always stock up with some canned versions of favourite fresh foods.

Before you set off on a shopping expedition, especially for a long trip, ask fellow crew members for their likes and dislikes. Keeping your crew well fed and contented will pay dividends!

Never underestimate the power of comfort foods. A simple bacon sandwich can work wonders by lifting the spirits of a cold, tired crew. And stock up with plenty of cakes, biscuits, chocolate bars and dried fruit and nuts. They can be devoured at an astonishing rate, especially on night watches.

Not all sailors are comfortable cooking in rough conditions, so when the weather threatens to take a turn for the worst, try and prepare meals in advance. Heating them up is simple and minimises the time spent below. The same applies before the start of a voyage. Excitement, tiredness and seasickness can take its toll during the first few days, so cook ahead if you can.

Quantities

Stocking up with exactly the right amount of food for a voyage can be tricky but these guidelines for fresh produce will help.

Ask the butcher to vacuum pack the meat in meal-sized portions. For instance, if your crew of six happen to be fond of beef stew (allowing 8oz of meat per person) then vacuum pack the meat in 3lb packs.

Poultry
An average chicken serves four people. Allow 225g (8oz) per person for chicken on the bone.

Lamb
Lamb stew: allow 275g (10oz) per person.
Leg: 1.4kg (3lb) for 3-4 people
    1.8kg (4lb) for 4-5 people
    2.7kg (6lb) for 7-8 people
Loin chops : 2 per person

Beef
Beef stew: 225g (8oz) per person
Roast beef: 200g (7oz) per person
Steaks: 200g-225g (7-8oz) per person
Minced meat: 175g (6oz) per person for hamburgers
    110g (4oz) for spaghetti, lasagne etc.

Veal
Stews: 225g (8oz) per person
Escalopes: 175g (6oz) per person

Pork
Pork stew: 175g (6oz) per person
Roast leg or loin off the bone 200g (7oz)
Chops 175g (6oz) chop per person

Bacon
Two slices, per person, per day

Fish
Large fish e.g. bass, tuna, salmon weighed whole, uncleaned: 340g–450g (12oz–1lb) per person

Shellfish
Allow 75g (3oz) as a first course, 150g (5oz) as a main course.

Rice
(Weighed before cooking)
Long grain and Risotto rice: 50g (2oz)

Vegetables
Allow 110g (4oz) of vegetables per person per meal, except for the following vegetables. (All these weights are calculated before preparation and cooking).
Green beans and peas: 75g (3oz)
Spinach: 350g (12oz)
Potatoes: Mashed 175g (6oz). New 110g (4oz)

Bread
A large loaf will generally make 20 slices

Butter
Allow 25g (1oz) of butter for 6 slices of bread

Milk
Allow 570ml (1 pint) for 20 cups of tea or coffee and 140ml ($\frac{1}{4}$ pint) for each portion of cereal.

Eggs
1 per person, per day.

Essential stores

The list below contains the basic items you will find useful to have in the store locker. To this you should add the ingredients for your own favourite recipes, as well as any in this cookbook.

Dried goods
Pasta: spaghetti, farfale, fettuccine, tagliatelli
Rice: long grain, wild rice, basmati and risotto
Beans: lentils, cannellini beans, split green peas, black beans
Dried mushrooms: porcini, cepes, morel
Sun dried tomatoes
Dried fruit and nuts, including raisins, walnuts and pine nuts
Muesli, porridge oats, cereals
Plain flour: (Do not overbuy, the shelf life is shorter than you think), dried yeast, self-raising flour, baking soda
Cake mixes, muffin mixes
Ground coffee, instant coffee
Tea bags including herbal teas of your choice
Cooking cognac
Granulated sugar, brown sugar, caster sugar
Dried milk and coffee whitener
Carrs water biscuits
Crisps/potato chips
Biscuits, chocolate bars, muesli bars
Stock cubes/granules
Herbs and spices: bay leaves, garlic (make sure you have plenty) dried mixed herbs, rosemary, thyme, coriander, celery salt, chilli powder, paprika, cumin, oregano, sea salt, peppercorns, curry powder

Sauces and bottled stores

Oils: Extra virgin olive oil, sesame oil, sunflower oil, walnut oil. Make sure you have plenty of olive oil, as the majority of the recipes contained in this book are cooked with virgin olive oil.

Vinegars: tarragon, balsamic, apple cider vinegar

Mustard: English and Dijon,

Sauces: Tabasco, pesto, soy, Worcestershire

Mayonnaise, tomato ketchup, horseradish, capers,

Jams, marmalade, honey, Marmite, peanut butter

Pickles and relishes

Canned goods

Tomatoes, tomato purée, sweetcorn, green beans, petits pois, mushrooms, tuna (canned in oil), sardines, anchovy fillets, bean sprouts, baked beans, red kidney beans, cannellini beans, chick peas, coconut milk, condensed milk, pâte, butter. In speciality delicatessen shops you should be able to buy cans of cassoulet or the equivalent Spanish fabadaba, which are meals in themselves.

Soups

Different varieties to taste, both canned and packet

Fresh produce

Meat, poultry and bacon

Selection of cold meats

Eggs

Fruit juices

Vegetables of choice, including salad vegetables

Dairy products

Fresh milk (in screw top, plastic bottles if possible), long life milk and cream, butter, (salted and unsalted), crème fraîche.

Cheeses

Soft cheeses have a short shelf life so look for the harder varieties such as Cheddar, Edam, Gouda, Emmental and Parmesan. Ready packed Feta cheese, which is delicious sprinkled on salads, and packaged Roquefort or blue cheese, have a surprisingly long shelf life of up to four months in the fridge.

Bread
There should be plenty of bread on board. It always seems to be consumed at a rapid pace when the going gets rough. Some supermarket bread will last a week. The German black bread lasts a month. Many supermarkets stock part-baked baguettes which do not require storage in the fridge and which last up to six weeks. If someone aboard enjoys baking bread there is nothing like the aroma of a freshly cooked loaf wafting through the hatch. Bread mixes are a good short-cut and give excellent results.

Convenience foods
When preparing for a longer trip, some convenience foods come into their own. The vacuum packed rosti potatoes served with scrambled eggs for breakfast are a 'must'. They do not need any preparation and are easy to store as they do not require any refrigeration. Vacuum packed pitta bread is also extremely useful. As previously mentioned, the part-baked baguettes sold in most supermarkets are well worth stocking. Quick and easy to prepare with a variety of fillings for lunch, they are also delicious served hot and crusty with soup on a cold day.

Freeze dried food – much favoured by those sailors who lean towards the 'dog bowl' approach to cooking afloat – is worth having in the store locker if you are planning a long trip, although I tend to think of it as 'survival food'.

Buy a few small cans of pâté. It is excellent served as a snack on Carrs water biscuits. These biscuits first appeared on ships in the late 19th century when it was found that using water, instead of fat, kept the biscuits fresher on long voyages. We also carry a couple of cans of foie gras for special occasions.

If you have not had time to make pesto sauce, or the ingredients are not available, then buy a couple of jars from a delicatessen or supermarket. The ready made pesto is nearly as good as the home made variety.

And look out for Gallo quick cook risotto rice which is available from good delicatessens. It can save a lot of cooking time.

Galley equipment

As space is at a premium, galley equipment should be selected carefully. Pots and pans should stack easily and dishes chosen of a type that can be used both on top of the stove and in the oven while looking presentable on the table.

Stoves
Gimbled stoves that run off camping gas are probably the best. Most galley stoves are difficult to regulate and thermostats are often unreliable, so use an oven thermometer and place it on the centre shelf of the oven to get a more accurate idea of the temperature.

Pots, pans and casseroles
Purchase good quality, heavy bottomed, stainless steel pots and pans (stainless steel does not rust). One of the best all-purpose casseroles is a heavy cast iron enamelled pot. Glazed earthenware dishes are also useful and contrary to many beliefs, survive being bounced around on the ocean waves. Both the cast iron and glazed earthenware have the advantage of being suitable for use on the top of the stove as well as in the oven. And they look good on the dining table.

Make sure you buy a saucepan large enough to boil pasta. A six-litre should be ample to serve six people. A pressure cooker is ideally suited to life on water. It can double up as a pasta pan, it cooks food far more speedily than conventional methods, thus saving energy, and you soon learn to appreciate the safety feature of cooking in a sealed container. It helps to ensure that an errant wake is not going to cause a messy disaster, even if the boat starts rocking excessively.

Frying pans
This is a matter of personal choice. Cast iron fying pans have to be treated with care and they are heavy to handle. I've found that non-stick pans are the best. They are inexpensive and once they have lost their non-stick surface, they can be abandoned to the rubbish bin. You will need two, but measure the top of the stove first to make sure they will fit the available space. Splatter screens, both small and large, are a good investment. They stop grease from spraying all over the galley.

Roasting tin
Instead of a tin, use a glazed earthenware dish or a shallow oval cast-iron gratin dish. Food can be served in these dishes direct to the table.

Bread tin, muffin tray and baking tray
Choose non-stick. They still have to be greased, but make it so much easier to turn out a clean end result. A bread tin can also double up as a cake tin.

Whisks
One balloon whisk and, (if you have the luxury of a generator), an electric hand whisk.

Knives
A set of good quality, stainless steel kitchen knives. I prefer the Swiss-made knives. They keep their edges well and are well worth the extra cost.

You will need two kitchen knives, one small and one medium sized, a good carving knife, a bread knife and a sharpening steel. And lastly, a filleting knife for those freshly caught fish.

A word of warning (and I speak from experience): do not let anyone, even the captain, borrow your knives for cutting ropes or allow them to be used as a replacement screwdriver!

Colander
Again, choose stainless steel as the plastic variety inevitably creates disaster when left too near the stove. Check the size of your sink, to make sure the colander will fit, and buy the largest one possible for draining pasta.

Salad dryer
The whirling variety that spins out the water is best. Using tea towels for drying lettuce is a non-starter, as they never seem to dry out properly at sea.

Spoons
A selection of wooden spoons, a ladle, a long-handled slotted and/or perforated draining spoon.

Measuring jug
Both metric and imperial with solid and liquid measurements.

U.S. Measuring Cups

Miscellaneous Items
Cheese grater. The four-sided variety is best if you have the space.
Cheese slicer, lemon squeezer (plastic), potato peeler, potato masher, can opener, corkscrew, bottle opener, scissors, funnel, garlic press, tongs, oven thermometer, sieve.

Kettle (with a whistle to economise on gas)

Thermos (to keep drinks hot during night watches)

Wooden chopping boards

Disposable items
Aluminium foil, self-seal plastic bags, large and small. Clingfilm, paper towels, paper plates, J-cloths or disposable dish cloths, plastic rubbish bags. Bio-fresh or 'Green' bags (see chapter on Storage) for storing fresh meat and vegetables.

Extravaganza
Consider investing in a blender. If you do not have a generator, 12-volt blenders are now available, from ship chandlers. Besides making sauces and soups, it is great for whipping up the odd cocktail. Another gadget worth having is a vacuum bag packer, especially if you do not have a freezer. Vacuum packed meat will last up to two weeks in the fridge and staples such as flour, rice, brown sugar and baking powder keep better when they are vacuum sealed. The packer can also be used outside the galley area for keeping tools and filters dry.

Storage

Efficient and well planned storage is one of the most important aspects of living aboard a boat. Space is at a premium and so the careful organisation of food and supplies is vital.

Once you have compiled your list of galley essentials, store them in a way that will allow you to locate them quickly and easily when needed. The where-on-earth-did-I-put-that scenario can all too frequently become the most frustrating part of cooking on a boat.

Each storage compartment on your boat should be numbered and each item inventoried as it is put away. Keep a master list of everything you put on board, note its exact location and mark it off the list as you use it so you know which items you are short of when you come to stocking up.

It is important to make sure that your most commonly used cooking utensils and ingredients are kept in the most easily accessible areas. It is also a good idea to keep smaller canisters or jars of the most regularly used items in the galley, refilling them from larger quantities stowed elsewhere.

The quality of most tinned and packet foods starts to deteriorate when stored for more than a year, so write the purchase date on your packages and cans with indelible ink. Discard any cans that show signs of leaking or that bulge.

Water

Most boats of over 50 feet have water makers aboard, so water storage for cooking and washing is not a problem. However, smaller boats do not have this facility and even boats with water makers have to provision for extra drinking water on Atlantic crossings or journeys that involve being at sea for over a week in the event of the water maker breaking down.

On average, allow five litres of drinking water per person, per day.

If there is a water shortage then vegetables may be boiled in clean saltwater. Add half an ounce of butter to the saucepan to prevent the water from boiling over.

Freezing

Freezers have a daily freezing capacity, this being the maximum volume of food that can be fast frozen in any 24 hours. Make a mental note that this is generally 10% of the total capacity of the freezer. Six hours is normally long enough to freeze most items. If you have a household freezer near to your boat, freeze items and then transfer them to your boat freezer. This saves batteries from being overloaded.

When preparing food for your freezer, measure out each meal with the quantity required. Sauces, stews and soups are best packaged in polythene bags, doubled up in case of leakage. Write the contents and storage date on the bag in chinagraph pencil or with a marker pen. Use different coloured labels for easy identification.

Make a list of the items you have frozen and tape the list to the lid or door of the freezer, crossing off items when you use them, so they can be replenished at the next port of call.

Meat should be cut into manageable or meal-sized portions and if possible de-boned to save space. Ask your butcher to vacuum pack the meat (or use your own vacuum packing machine). All vacuum packed fresh meat will last up to two weeks in the fridge.

If you are unable to vacuum pack the meat, place it in a polythene bag, withdraw all the air with a straw and fasten with a twist tie. If the bones remain on the meat, wrap them in foil to avoid package damage in the freezer.

Poultry and game should be washed inside and out and dried. Note that giblets have a far shorter freezer life (two months).

Fish and shellfish freeze well but must be packaged carefully or they will contaminate surrounding food.

If you decide to freeze fish in steak-size portions, place a layer of foil or cling film between each portion before wrapping them again in cling film. Overwrap with foil and seal well before labelling and freezing.

Beef, lamb, veal and chicken will keep in the freezer for up to one year and pork between three and six months. Frozen food will not turn bad, but will eventually lose its flavour as time goes by.

The best way to defrost food is in the refrigerator. Defrosted food will spoil quicker, so use as soon as possible.

Any unpackaged hams or cooked meats can be vacuum packed and kept in the fridge.

If you are unlucky enough to experience a power failure, or if the freezer or fridge breaks down, bear in mind that the contents of a fully loaded freezer will stay frozen for up to two days, as long as it remains unopened. If the breakdown looks as if it will last more than a day, try to get hold of some ice or dry ice. When using dry ice, be sure to wear gloves and do not place directly onto the food, but on a piece of cardboard first.

Canned goods
Canned goods should be stored in a cool dry place. When storing cans in the bilge, remove the labels and colour code or number them instead (keeping a master list). Varnish or spray the tins to prevent rusting. Once a can has been opened, transfer the contents into a fresh container and store in the refrigerator. Use within 48 hours.

Dairy produce

If possible buy butter in a can. Some of the Dutch and Normandy butters are sold in this way, with a removable plastic lid. These can be stored in a cool place outside of the fridge until required. Buy salted butter, as it keeps longer than the unsalted variety.

Long life milk can also be stored in a cool place until required, but once opened should be kept in the fridge. Whenever possible buy the long life milk that comes in a container with a screw top. Milk in a carton has the unfortunate habit of tipping over once opened. A smelly fridge in a rough sea is not a pleasant experience!

You will probably not have enough room in your fridge for storing eggs but they can safely be kept in a cool area for up to three weeks, if purchased really fresh. Should you be embarking on a long journey, it is especially important to know whether the eggs you have bought are really fresh. To check, place the egg in a bowl of cold water. If it lies at the bottom in a horizontal position it is very fresh. If it tilts slightly, it is semi fresh and if the egg goes into a vertical position it is definitely stale.

Fruit

Apples and oranges may be stored for up to two to three weeks. Sacrifice a well-ventilated locker. We found our aft lazarette serves well.

Store the fruit in a box, placing paper towel between each layer. A towel should be placed over the top layer to absorb humidity.

Melons should be well wrapped in a polythene bag, before being put in the fridge, as the odour penetrates other food.

Do not make the mistake of buying too many bananas, as they ripen simultaneously. For a long distance voyage with a large crew, buy a hand of green bananas and suspend it in the cabin.

Soft fruit should not be bought in any quantity. It goes off very quickly and normally there is not enough room to store it in the fridge. Soft fruit also tends to attract fruit flies.

Vegetables

Most vacuum packed vegetables, such as beans, courgettes and aubergines, will last up to two weeks in the fridge, sometimes longer.

Alternatively, buy long-life produce-storage bags that eliminate bacteria and double the lifetime of fruit, vegetables, meat and fish. These are produced by Evert-Fresh in the U.S. and known as Green Bags or bio bags. The colour of the bag cuts the ultra-violet rays of light that cause produce to ripen. Contact: www.evert-fresh.com

Green tomatoes, stored in the fridge, will last well over two weeks. Bring them out to ripen when required. Onions, potatoes and carrots should be stored in an airy locker, again placing paper towels between each layer. On a long trip, check occasionally to see that none of the items have gone mouldy, as one bad potato will soon contaminate your whole locker.

Salad

Wash, dry well and put into a zip lock bag or a Green Bag. This is where a spinning salad dryer comes in very useful. You may be able to purchase ready packed and sealed little gem or iceberg lettuces that will last up to two weeks. Alternatively, vacuum pack your lettuces and they will last up to three weeks.

Dried foods

Find the driest locker for storing this type of food. Place in plastic containers or in self-seal bags. This will prevent humidity from affecting the food. Do not be tempted to buy too much flour. It has a shorter shelf life than you may think, especially in the damp atmosphere aboard. Normally allow three months for white flour and two months for wholewheat flour. Mark the containers with the purchase date.

A good tip is to place a bay leaf in your dried pasta or flour, as this cuts the risk of being invaded by weevils.

This brings us to the question of other invasions. After you have bought your produce for the trip, and invariably loaded all the items into various cardboard boxes to transport back to your boat, *do not, under any circumstances*, load the cardboard boxes on to your boat. They are the worst breeding sites for cockroaches, this being the most common way these particularly unwelcome vermin get on board. Once aboard, cockroaches breed at a frightening rate and are almost impossible to get rid of. Collapsible plastic boxes are widely available. Take them with you to the supermarket and pack your purchases directly into them. This will help to ensure that you bring everything back to the boat cockroach-free.

On longer journeys, when more storage space is required, nets can be hung in strategic places. These are very convenient for storing avocados and for ripening tomatoes or bananas. Any salamis or hams can be hung in an appropriate place – preferably somewhere where they don't bang passing heads.

Facing page: La Ratatouille Niçoise (page 154) with Gratin Dauphinois (page 151) and Gigot d'Agneau à la Moutarde (page 123).

MENU PLANS

When planning a trip, whether for a weekend or a transatlantic voyage, it is essential to plan your menus in advance. Estimate how long your longest passage is likely to be – and add a further 20 per cent.

To give you some ideas, this chapter features some of my menu plans and diary for two trips we have undertaken in recent years – a four day sail with a crew of five, from Menorca to Gibraltar and our first ARC (Atlantic Race for Cruisers) race, a 16-day voyage from Las Palmas in the Canary Islands to St. Lucia in the Caribbean.

I haven't included breakfasts as these will almost certainly consist of the usual sailor's fare – a variation of eggs, croissants, fruit and cereals, etc. However, you will find some suggestions for egg-based meals in the chapter on Eggs.

Menorca to Gibraltar

(Four days)

Day One: 29th October
At last we've set sail, destination Gibraltar. Will plan Goulash for tonight. Cooked the Goulash but the cook is not feeling too good, so prepared everything and left the others to it. Slightly rough sea.

Lunch
Bean Salad
Green salad
Mixed Cold Meats, Ham, Salami, etc.
Cheese with Fresh Bread from the local bakery

Dinner
Goulash with Farfalle and Courgettes
Apples Baked with Raisins

Day Two: 30th October
Still a bit rough so plan sandwiches and soup for lunch. Plenty of different cold meats on board for sandwiches.
Probably best to plan for some sort of pasta dish for this evening's meal.

Lunch
Sandwiches
Hot Vichyssoise

Dinner
Tagliatelle with Mushrooms
Green Salad
Cheese and Biscuits

Day Three: 31st October

Weather improving, so we have a celebration with Jupiter Moon's infamous Bloody Marys and JT's scrumptious brunch with eggs, fried potatoes and sausages.Inspired by the Bloody Marys we manage to catch two tuna fish to barbecue. This turns out to be quite a perilous exercise, which I promise not to undertake again under sail. However, the tuna is quite delicious, especially with the Ratatouille that I had made earlier in the day.

Brunch
Bloody Marys
Scrambled Eggs
Fried Potatoes and Sausages

Dinner
Marinated Tuna Steaks
Ratatouille
Fresh fruit

Day Four: 1st November

Celebration day as it is JT's birthday. We should be in Gibraltar to celebrate tonight, so put the champagne in the fridge and make some Guacamole and Houmous as appetisers for this evening.We still have tuna left from the fish Rohan caught yesterday –so it's Ceviche for lunch.

Lunch
Ceviche with Salad and Hot Baguette
Fresh fruit

Evening
Champagne with appetisers of Guacamole and Houmous with Pitta Bread

Dinner *in port*

Las Palmas to St. Lucia

(16 days)

Day 1: November 24th
09.00 Last minute shopping. Decks washed, stores all away, shopping finished, sigh of relief.Everyone getting ready for departure.

13.00 Good start – holding tenth place. Open bottles of Champagne, served with Foie Gras and Smoked Salmon. The first of many celebrations.

Dinner
Had already prepared tonight's meal – Blanquette de Veau – a few days ago on shore, as knew it would be a hectic day and I wouldn't have time to think about cooking.

Blanquette de Veau with Rice and Green Beans
Salad
Pastries bought in the market

Day 2: November 25th
Compass course: 217 degrees. Not much wind today, but we have made 140 miles since our departure.

Lunch
Only our second day out so decided to make the most of recently purchased fresh vegetables.

Salad Niçoise
Hot Baguettes

P.M. *Relatively calm, prepare Goulash for tomorrow's evening meal.*

Dinner
Chicken Tarragon with Lemon
Green Beans and Potatoes
Fresh Fruit

Day 3: November 26th
Course now 260 degrees. Haven't seen any other boats. Genoa and full main. Wind NE 8 knots. We've put the fishing lines out – and are now making pancakes for breakfast.
A bit chilly, so make Minestrone soup for lunch.

Lunch
Minestrone with Hot Baguettes
Green Salad and Cheese

P.M. *As Goulash already prepared, have time to make American Fruit Pie with apples for dessert.*

Dinner
Goulash with Potatoes and Broccoli
American Fruit Pie

Day 4: November 27th
Exciting day. Wing and wing up to 12.9 knots. Saw killer whale starboard jumping out of the water. We made 184 miles in the last 24 hours. Time for a celebration, so pulled out a bottle of Champagne.

Lunch
Piedmontese Pepperoni with Mixed Cold Meats
   (Mortadella, Proscuitto, Ham)
Hot Crusty Bread

Dinner
Gigot d'Agneau à la Moutarde
Dauphinois Potatoes
Baked Apples with Raisins

Day Five: November 28th

Weather a bit warmer - longitude 26.05 West. We are past Cape Verde Islands. Saw a bird flying around. Wind now easterly, on 6-7 knots. Take out prawns from freezer make a lunchtime salad as rocket/arugula leaves starting to look a little tired.

Lunch
Proscuitto
Prawns, Parmesan and Rocket Salad
Baguettes

Getting rough so decide to make Spaghetti Carbonara for tonight's dinner.

Dinner
Spaghetti Carbonara
Green Salad
Fresh Fruit

Day 6: November 29th

Course 249 degrees. Running under reefed main and shortened genoa. Sloppy seas, fishing lines out - at last caught a tuna for dinner - great.
Galley not very conducive to cooking at the moment, but will throw together a salad of Tabbouleh with some cold meats.

Lunch
Cold Meats with Tabbouleh

P.M. *Seas calmer now, prepare Bolognese Sauce and put in freezer in case we get into more bad weather.*

Dinner
Tuna Steaks with Red Onions and Balsamic Vinegar
Rice
Apple Crumble

Day 7: November 30th

*Compass course 270 degrees. Problem with generator – start battery dead.
Jump started with mains battery. Little concerned about the fridge and its
contents, but all's well.*

Take spinach from freezer for lunch.

Lunch
Catalan Spinach with Hard Boiled Eggs and Baguettes

*P.M. Notice a couple of avocados are getting rather ripe, ideal for a Guacamole.
Looks as if we may be in for a storm, so will defrost Bolognese Sauce.*

*There is a heavy squall. Rain means visibility not good. Ripped out outer reef
point on No. 3 reef. This was mended in record time between snacks of
Guacamole. A very hungry tired crew eagerly finish off the Spaghetti Bolognese
in record time.*

Dinner
Guacamole
Spaghetti Bolognese

Day 8: December 1st

*Course 249 degrees.Woke up to clear skies and barometer going up so crew are
in good spirits. Spoke on VHF radio to a Guadaloupe-bound catamaran two
miles to starboard.*

Lunch
Puy Lentil Salad
Cold Meats and Hot Crusty Bread

Dinner
Pot Roasted Veal with Farfalle
Fruit and Ice Cream

Day 9: December 2nd

Compass course 251 degrees. Wind fell from 7.2 to 6.8 knots in last four hours. Mean average 7.1 knots - 1360 miles covered. The half way point! Celebration - out with the Champagne. Spirits high. Take out chicken fillets from freezer for dinner.

Lunch
Courgette and Lemon Soup
Bread, Cheese and Fruit

Dinner
Chicken with Mushrooms and Garlic
Potatoes and Green Beans
Guava with Cream Cheese

Day 10: December 3rd

Cloudy, cold and damp. Where is paradise? But have averaged 8 knots over last five hours.Will make lentil soup for lunch to warm the crew up. Heavy squall, rain, visibility 10 metres. Ripped out outer reef point at No. 3 reef again. All repaired. 27 miles in three hours. Take out lamb from freezer.

Lunch
Lentil Soup with Sausages
Hot Bread

Dinner
Lamb Braised in Red Wine and Vinegar
Broccoli and Potatoes
Ricotta and Marscapone Cream

Day 11: December 4th
Clear sky this morning, at last barometer going up and sea calmer. Flying fish land regularly on deck.

Lunch
Frittata with Onions and Sun Dried Tomatoes
Baguette
Fruit and Cheese

P.M. *Very calm, will make the Jupiter Moon Nutty Fruit Cake for supper.*

Dinner
Fettucine with Walnut Sauce
Green Salad
Jupiter Moon Nutty Fruit Cake

Day 12: December 5th
A few showers. Put up Yankee with genoa. 6.6 knots. Saw a whale jumping out of the water, one mile off starboard. Loads of flying fish land on the deck. Rohan caught a tuna, so will have Ceviche for lunch.

Lunch
Ceviche with Baguettes
Salad
Fruit

P.M. *Relatively calm sea, Rohan preparing crêpe mixture for tonight's dessert.*

Dinner
Osso Bucco Milanese with Rice
Courgettes
Crêpes

Day 13: December 6th

Making good time with two genoas poled out. Then bearings loose on deck from genoa rewind drum – jury repair, pin was replaced on genoa stay.
Tomatoes getting rather ripe and need to be eaten, so will roast them with Mozzarella for lunch. Take out Poussin from freezer for tonight's dinner.

Lunch
Roasted Tomatoes with Mozzarella
Cold Meats and Baguettes

Make American Fruit Pie with dried apricots and slivered almonds for dinner.

Dinner
Poussin au Citron
Glazed Carrots
Rice
American Fruit Pie

Day 14: December 7th

Average today 6.9 knots. Not good but steady and comfortable. Take loin of pork out of the freezer which will roast tonight. Make brownies for dessert.

Lunch
Soupe à l'Oignon
Hot Crusty Baguette

Dinner
Rôti de Porc
Rice and Peas
Jean's Brownies with Ice Cream

Day 15: December 8th

Crew getting excited as we are nearing our destination. First boats have arrived in Rodney Bay. Will finish off the last of the tomatoes and avocados for lunch. As we are getting closer to St. Lucia decide to make a Caribbean dish, so take chicken from freezer.

Lunch
Tomatoes, Mozzarella and Avocado Salad
Cold Meats and Baguettes

Dinner
Fricassée de Poulet de Coco et Quince
Rice and Peas
Ice Cream

Day 16: December 10th

Very sudden squall this morning. 35 knots.
Sloppy seas, sails banging around – only 154.4 miles to go! Will make pasta for lunch, with luck we may be eating ashore tonight.

Lunch
Fettucine with Roquefort Cheese
Endive Salad

We arrive in Rodney Bay to be met by a heavy rain squall and the ARC officials bearing delicious – and very welcome – rum punches. The celebrations begin!

Total: 2,426 miles.

Facing page: Courgette (Zucchini) and Lemon Soup (page 53).

SOUP

Soup is a vital element on board a boat. Dried and canned soups should be kept in the store locker for stormy weather conditions. Always make sure you have a selection of different varieties to suit all tastes. In normal sailing conditions, soup and a sandwich constitute a healthy balanced lunch, while a really hearty soup with pasta thrown in, and followed by cheese and salad, makes a tasty, satisfying supper.

You may not have the space in your freezer to keep stock, but if you do, making it is both easy and rewarding. A large quantity can be made and used at a later date, as it freezes perfectly. Alternatively, if you do not have a freezer, stock can be stored in the fridge in a covered container for up to four days.

Although a good fresh stock is the basis for all the best soups, it is not always practical to make when sailing. For these occasions there are a number of concentrated stock cubes and extremely tasty vegetarian granules on the market that are suitable for boat life.

A pressure cooker for making soup can save time and gas, especially with some of the bean recipes. I would also recommend purchasing a 12 volt electric blender. This is a wonderful tool for whipping up delicious soups in half the time.

Vegetable Stock

Vegetable stock can be made from any type of vegetables. The following is a basic recipe to which you can add a variety of vegetables.

2 tablespoons of olive oil
2 small onions chopped
5 sliced carrots
3 sticks of celery washed and chopped
2 fennel bulbs chopped
1 bouquet garni
2 tablespoons of black peppercorns
4 bay leaves
2 litres/3^1/2 pints of water

Heat the oil in a large saucepan, gently fry the onions until soft, add the chopped carrots, celery and fennel and fry until slightly brown. Add the water and the rest of the ingredients, bring to a boil and simmer for one hour, then strain.

Chicken Stock

Ideally use fresh chicken trimmings or a medium size chicken, having removed the meat for use in another recipe.

Bones of a 1.5kg chicken
2 celery sticks
2 carrots
1 onion peeled and cut in two
2 bay leaves
2 sprigs of thyme
1 teaspoon black peppercorns
3 litres/5^1/4 pints of cold water

Put all the ingredients into a large saucepan, bring to the boil and simmer very gently for an hour. Strain.

Lentil Soup

A classic dish which goes down well on cold, wet nights. It freezes well and is always tastier the next day. It can also be made in a pressure cooker. Another option is to add pasta at the end.

Serves four

225g/8oz Puy lentils
400g/14oz can chopped tomatoes
3 tablespoons of olive oil
1 onion, finely chopped
110g/4oz diced bacon
2 sticks of celery, chopped
2 cloves of garlic, peeled and chopped
1.7 litres/3 pints chicken stock
175g/6oz pasta (optional)
Salt and freshly ground pepper

Heat the olive oil in a large saucepan and sauté the bacon, onion, garlic and celery until the onion is slightly brown. Meanwhile rinse and drain the lentils and stir them into the pan so that they absorb the oil and bacon fat. Add the chopped tomatoes and the chicken stock. Season and simmer for about one hour. When the lentils are tender you may add the pasta (optional) and cook until *al dente*. Season and serve.

If using a pressure cooker:
Heat the olive oil in the cooker and follow as above. After adding the chopped tomatoes and chicken stock, lock the lid in place and cook for twenty minutes at high pressure. Let the pressure drop naturally or use the quick release method.

Lentil Soup with Italian Sausages

Serves four

Follow instructions for Lentil Soup (page 46). At the same time as you are sautéing the bacon, onion, garlic and celery, cook 8 Italian sausages (if not available, any sausages of choice) until golden brown. Add to the bacon, onion, garlic and celery and drained lentils, along with the chopped tomatoes and chicken stock. Cook for one hour.

Season and serve.

Vichyssoise

A favourite soup for most people. Depending on the season, it can be served hot or cold.

Serves four

4 leeks chopped, discard the green leaves
3 potatoes, peeled and chopped
2 onions, finely chopped
25g/1oz butter
750ml/1 1/4 pints chicken stock
250ml/9 fl oz cream
2 tablespoons of freshly chopped chives or chopped parsley
Salt and freshly ground black pepper

Melt the butter and add the chopped leeks, onions and cook over a low flame until soft. Add the chopped potatoes to the leeks and onions and pour in the stock.* Cover and simmer for 30 minutes or until vegetables are cooked. Purée with either a sieve or a blender. Return the soup to the stove and heat gently before adding the cream, salt and pepper.

Sprinkle with the chopped chives or parsley.

* If using a pressure cooker, secure the lid at this point, and cook for five minutes. Let the pressure drop naturally, then liquidise in a blender or sieve the contents and continue as above.

Minestrone

This is a very hearty soup as well as being versatile. You can add a variety of different vegetables according to what you may have in your store locker and/or fridge.

Serves four

2 tablespoons of olive oil
2 medium size onions, finely chopped
2 carrots, chopped
110g/4oz of prosciutto or unsmoked bacon, chopped
2 teaspoons of dried sage
1 clove of garlic, peeled and finely chopped
2 courgettes(zuccini) cut into thin strips
2 potatoes, peeled and diced
1 stick of celery, diced
1.7 litres/3 pints of vegetable or chicken stock
400g/14oz can of chopped tomatoes
400g/14oz can of chick peas or haricot beans
150g/5oz pasta
Grated Parmesan cheese
Salt and freshly ground pepper

Heat the oil in a large casserole or saucepan. Sauté the prosciutto or bacon until it starts to colour, then add the onions, garlic, carrots, potatoes, celery and sage. Sauté until the onions start to brown. Add the tomatoes, courgettes and the stock. Bring to the boil and simmer covered for about two hours. After two hours add the chickpeas or haricot beans and the pasta. Season and cook until the pasta is al dente.

Remove from the heat and stir in the Parmesan. Serve hot.

Soupe à l'Oignon

After a trip there always seems to be a glut of onions, so the traditional onion soup is an enjoyable way to make use of them. This is a hearty meal in itself.

Serves six

8 medium onions, thinly sliced
4 tablespoons of butter
1 litre/2½ pints beef or vegetable stock
110ml/4fl oz cognac (optional)
6 rounds toasted French bread
225g/8oz grated Gruyère cheese
1 teaspoon sugar
Salt and pepper

Heat the butter and sugar in a large heavy saucepan. Add the onions and cook very gently over a low flame, stirring constantly until the onions are golden brown. Add the stock slowly and stir until the soup starts to boil. Cover and simmer gently for one hour.

Before serving, add the cognac, salt and pepper. Pour the soup into bowls and place a round of toasted French bread covered with freshly grated Gruyère cheese on the top.

Black Bean Soup with Crème Fraîche

A marvellous soup which originated in Spain and became popular in Cuba. Thick, black and utterly delicious...

Serves six

250g/9oz black beans
2 tablespoons of olive oil
3 onions, finely chopped
110g/4oz chopped bacon
400g/14oz can chopped tomatoes
2 cloves of garlic, finely chopped
1 carrot, finely chopped
1 stick celery, finely chopped
1 teaspoon ground coriander
2 teaspoons ground cumin
1.2 litres/2 pints chicken stock
3 tablespoons crème fraîche or whipped cream (optional)
Salt and freshly ground pepper

Soak the beans overnight. Drain and rinse with fresh water.

Heat the olive oil in a large casserole and add the bacon. Cook for five minutes. Add the onions, garlic, carrot, celery, cumin and coriander. Lower the heat and cook for a further ten minutes. Add the drained black beans, stirring so they absorb the oil. After a few minutes pour in the stock. Season with salt and pepper* and simmer very gently for three hours, stirring from time to time.

When the soup is ready you can either serve it as it is, or purée it, using a blender or sieve. Reheat gently and serve with a dollop of crème fraîche or cream.

*If using a pressure cooker, adjust the heat to maintain a high pressure. Cook for 35 minutes. Let the pressure drop naturally, or use the quick release method. Continue as above.

Green Pea Soup

A wonderfully hearty, warming and comforting soup...

Serves four

2 tablespoons olive oil
2 onions, finely chopped
350g/12oz dried green peas, soaked overnight
2 litres/3¹/2 pints chicken stock
2 stalks celery, finely chopped
110g/4oz bacon, finely chopped
Salt and freshly ground black pepper

Heat the oil in a large saucepan and sauté the onions, bacon and celery. Drain the peas from their soaking liquid, then add them to the pan along with the chicken stock.* Simmer covered for two to three hours, adding more water if the soup becomes too thick.

When cool put the soup through a blender, then reheat and season with salt and pepper.

* If using a pressure cooker, lock the lid in place and maintain high pressure for ten minutes. Let pressure drop naturally.

Courgette (Zucchini) and Lemon Soup

Courgette, or zucchini or squash, is a useful vegetable to have aboard. Depending on the variety, their shelf life can be up to two weeks and they can be made into a very refreshing summer soup when combined with lemon juice.

Serves four

450g/1lb courgettes, finely chopped
1 medium sized red onion, sliced
2 tablespoons olive oil
Zest and juice of one large lemon
570ml/1 pint chicken stock
2 egg yolks
1 small tub plain yoghurt
Salt and freshly ground black pepper

Heat the oil in a large saucepan and sauté the onion until it becomes transparent. Add the courgettes and gently cook for a further four minutes. Add the lemon zest and juice, chicken stock and seasoning. Cover and simmer for about 20 minutes. Cool, then purée in a blender. Beat the egg yolks and yoghurt together and then add to the soup. Heat gently, stirring continuously until all the ingredients have been amalgamated.

This soup may be served hot or cold. If served cold, slice a courgette and decorate each bowl.

Spicy Chickpea Soup

This soup will warm the cockles of any sailor's heart. A store locker recipe that can be produced very quickly and with the minimum of effort.

Serves four

450g/14oz can of chickpeas
50g/2oz butter
2 teaspoons ground cumin
2 teaspoons ground coriander
4 cloves of garlic, peeled and chopped
1 small dried chilli, seeds removed and chopped
570ml/1 pint vegetable stock
Crème fraîche or whipping cream
Salt and freshly ground pepper

Put the chickpeas and their liquid in a saucepan and heat gently for five minutes. Remove from the heat. Meanwhile, heat the butter in a frying pan, add the garlic and cook gently for a few minutes until the garlic turns golden brown. Add the ground coriander and cumin powder and continue cooking over a low heat for a further three minutes.

Blend or sieve the chickpeas and the spices together until smooth. Return the contents to the saucepan with the vegetable stock and seasoning. Simmer for 20 minutes, stirring from time to time.

Serve with crème fraîche or whipping cream.

Facing page: Green Bean Salad with Cheese, Lemon and Mint (page 62).

SALADS
STARTERS AND APPETISERS

From our many summers spent cruising the Mediterranean, we found that salads were an obvious choice for a lunchtime menu. When fresh produce is readily available, it is not difficult to conjure up something quite delicious. Some of the following recipes are very simple ideas based on ingredients that you may have in your fridge or store locker. Included is the classic Salad Niçoise – it really does makes a perfect lunch dish.

Guacamole

A favourite appetiser aboard *Jupiter Moon* and one that comes in very useful when the avocados are too soft to use for anything else!

2 ripe avocados
Juice of 1/2 lemon
1 clove garlic, mashed
1/2 red onion, finely chopped
1 tablespoon of chopped parsley (optional)
2 tablespoons of olive oil
Salt and freshly ground black pepper

Peel and mash the avocados with a fork (a blender will make it too creamy). Add the lemon juice, crushed garlic, onion and parsley, then slowly add the olive oil and salt and pepper to taste.

Leave the avocado stones in the mixture until you are ready to serve as this stops the avocado from turning brown.

Houmous

Another great appetiser. Remember to buy pitta bread for your store locker to serve with the houmous. Also stock up with tahini available at health food shops.

250g of chickpeas (bottled or canned variety)
2 tablespoons of tahini
2 large cloves of garlic, peeled and chopped
2 tablespoons of virgin olive oil
1 handful of parsley, finely chopped

Mash the chickpeas then add the tahini, garlic, virgin olive oil and parsley, combine well together. Alternatively put all the ingredients into a blender.

Serve cold with pitta bread.

Roasted Tomatoes with Mozzarella

Serves four

8 large tomatoes (on the vine if possible)
2 tablespoon of olive oil
2 cloves of garlic, peeled and chopped
1 small bunch of basil
2 tablespoons of balsamic vinegar
225g/8oz mozzarella cheese
Salt and freshly ground pepper

Preheat the oven to 200°C/400°F/Gas Mark 6

Pour boiling water over the tomatoes, leave them for no longer than one minute, and then skin them when they are cool enough to handle. Cut the tomatoes in half and place in a shallow earthenware dish or shallow roasting tin, season with salt and pepper and sprinkle with the chopped garlic and a little olive oil.

Roast the tomatoes in the oven for about 40 minutes or until they are slightly browned at the edge. Meanwhile, slice the mozzarella and place a slice on each tomato. Return to the oven until the mozzarella has melted. Just before serving, drizzle balsamic vinegar and then virgin olive oil over the tomatoes and mozzarella. Season with salt and pepper.

Serve with ciabatta bread, or any crusty bread that is available.

Piedmontese Pepperoni

This is the classic dish from Piedmont, in Italy. Quick and easy to make, it is equally delicious as a starter or as a salad.

Serves four

2 red peppers and 2 yellow peppers cut in half lengthways and
seeds removed.
4 tablespoons olive oil
4 tomatoes, skins removed
8 anchovy fillets,
2 cloves of garlic, peeled and sliced
1 bunch of basil (optional)
Salt and freshly ground pepper

Preheat the oven to 180°C/ 350°F/Gas Mark 4

Lightly oil a baking dish. Place the peppers in the dish and into each half put 2 or 3 slices of garlic, half a tomato cut in two, and an anchovy fillet cut into pieces. Lightly drizzle with olive oil. Roast for about thirty minutes, making sure the peppers do not overcook. They should be reasonably firm when you remove them.

Serve cold garnished with basil.

Puy Lentil Salad with Olive Oil

Use Puy lentils if you can, they are the crème de la crème of the lentil family. Store lentils in your locker, but make sure to keep an eye on their sell-by date. People often believe that because they are dried they will last forever. In fact, the fresher they are the better they taste.

Serves four to six

300g/11oz Puy lentils
1 onion, peeled and quartered
1 bouquet garni
4 tablespoons of virgin olive oil
1 red chilli pepper, de-seeded and finely chopped
2 tablespoons parsley
1 red or white onion, finely chopped
Salt and freshly ground pepper

Vinaigrette
1 tablespoon of wine vinegar
3 tablespoons of virgin olive oil
1/2 teaspoon honey
1 clove of garlic, finely chopped
Salt and pepper

Rinse the lentils then cover with cold water. Add the quartered onion and bouquet garni and simmer for 30 minutes until the lentils are cooked but still firm. Drain, then remove the onion and bouquet garni. While the lentils are still warm add the olive oil, chilli pepper, salt and pepper. Leave to cool.

Before serving, add the chopped onion and the vinaigrette. Garnish with the parsley.

Green Bean Salad with Cheese, Lemon and Mint

A wonderfully refreshing salad, suitable as a starter or a light lunch. I like to use lots of garlic and leave it in the fridge with the vinaigrette for an hour or so. It really improves the flavour of the salad.

Serves four

250g/8oz fine green beans, halved
2 courgettes(zucchini), cut in small quarters
200g/7oz fresh or frozen peas
200g/7oz mozzarella or feta cheese
4 tablespoons of mint, finely chopped
4 slices of ciabatta or crusty bread
2 cloves of garlic, finely chopped
8 anchovy fillets, chopped

Vinaigrette dressing
Juice of one lemon
2 teaspoons of Dijon mustard
2 teaspoons of honey
9 tablespoons of olive oil

Top and tail the beans. Place in boiling, salted water. Parboil for four minutes, then add the courgettes (zucchini) for another minute. Drain and immediately place under cold running water to halt the cooking process. Add the peas to the water and cook until tender. Drain and cool.

Meanwhile, make the vinaigrette, putting the lemon juice in the salad bowl with the honey and mustard, mix well then slowly add the olive oil to make a creamy dressing.

Combine all the ingredients with the chopped garlic and anchovy fillets. Season with salt and pepper. Pour the vinaigrette over the salad.

Cut the mozzarella into small cubes or crumble the feta cheese and add it to the salad along with the chopped mint.

Serve with ciabatta or crusty bread.

Bean Salad

Another light and refreshing salad which also benefits from being left in the fridge with the vinaigrette dressing for an hour or so before serving.

Serves four

700g/1 1/2lb of fine green beans
1 handful of chopped parsley
4 cloves of garlic, peeled and finely chopped

Vinaigrette dressing: see recipe on page 176

Top and tail the beans. Cook in boiling salted water until barely tender. Strain and immediately place under cold running water to make sure the cooking process stops. Add the vinaigrette, chopped garlic and parsley. Mix well. Chill and serve.

Pasta Salad with Smoked Salmon and Lemon

Keep a small vacuum pack of smoked salmon in the fridge, it will keep for over a month and makes a useful store locker item to be used either in salads or pasta, or simply on toast for a treat.

When cooking pasta for a salad, do not cook it too far in advance as it tends to dry out quite quickly.

Serves four

250g/8oz of smoked salmon
400g/14oz farfalle or pasta twists
3 tablespoons lemon juice
6 tablespoons olive oil
1 clove garlic, peeled and chopped (optional)
Salt and freshly ground pepper

Cook the pasta in a large quantity of boiling water. Strain and rinse with cold water. Add the chopped garlic, lemon juice and olive oil, then season with salt and pepper. Leave to cool. Cut the salmon into strips and gently mix with the pasta.

Prosciutto, Prawns, Parmesan and Rocket Salad

This is a delightful combination. If rocket (known as arugula in the U.S) is not available, then use a mixture of parsley and mixed salad leaves. A great cockpit salad for one of those relaxing, hot, sunny days. Serve it with an ice-cold bottle of white wine and ciabatta bread – or any crusty bread available.

Serves four

8 slices very thin prosciutto
110g/4oz peeled prawns, either fresh or frozen variety
110g/4oz rocket, or salad leaves mixed with parsley
1 clove garlic, peeled and finely chopped
4 tablespoons virgin olive oil
1 tablespoon balsamic vinegar
110g/4oz Parmesan shavings (Use a cheese slicer or potato peeler)
Salt and freshly ground pepper

Place the rocket or salad on a large plate. Tear the prosciutto into pieces and arrange between the leaves. Scatter the prawns on top.

Make a vinaigrette dressing by mixing the garlic, olive oil and balsamic vinegar and pour over the salad. Add the Parmesan shavings. Finally, grind over some black pepper and serve.

Mushrooms à la Grècque

A delicious and tasty dish which can be prepared in advance. Serve it chilled, either as a starter or salad.

Serves four

225g/8oz of small mushrooms
12 tiny white onions peeled (if unavailable, use 4 ordinary white
  onions quartered)
1/2 wine glass white wine
1/2 wine glass olive oil
1 wine glass vegetable or chicken stock
1 tablespoon tomato paste
1 tablespoon whole peppercorns
Salt, bay leaf
Paprika

Wash and then drain the mushrooms. Put all the ingredients except the paprika into a saucepan. Simmer for forty minutes, uncovered. Allow to cool before putting it in the fridge. Serve cold, sprinkled with paprika.

Serve with ciabatta or crusty bread.

Tabbouleh

Burghul wheat is a very useful ingredient to have on board. It only needs to be soaked for fifteen minutes and provides the base for Tabbouleh, a delicious Middle Eastern dish usually served with cold chicken or other cold meats.

Serves four

110g/4oz burghul (cracked) wheat
2 tomatoes, chopped
1/2 cucumber, finely chopped
6 spring/salad onions or 1 red onion, finely chopped
1 large handful fresh mint, finely chopped
1 large handful parsley, finely chopped.
3 tablespoons virgin olive oil
Salt and freshly ground black pepper
Lemon juice

Soak the wheat for fifteen minutes in cold water. Drain and put into a clean tea towel to soak up the excess moisture. Mix all the other ingredients together in a bowl, before adding the burghul wheat, lemon juice and salt and pepper to taste. The lemon juice and mint are very important if you are to bring out the true flavour of Tabbouleh.

Salad Niçoise

This is the classic and dependable Salad Niçoise, ideal for serving on board, as all the ingredients can be combined in one bowl. And it also looks delicious!

Serves four

1 medium size can of tuna fish (in olive oil if possible)
250g/9oz of green beans cooked *al dente*
2 small lettuces, torn into pieces
1 sweet green pepper, chopped
2 celery stalks, chopped
8 anchovy fillets
4 hard boiled eggs, quartered
8 black olives
4 tomatoes, quartered
1 red onion, chopped

Vinaigrette dressing: see page 176

In a wooden (if possible) salad bowl prepare the vinaigrette dressing then add all the above ingredients except the egg, tuna fish and anchovies. Just before you serve the salad, toss the ingredients well, then top with the tuna fish, eggs and anchovies.

Serve with fresh baguette.

EGGS

Eggs are synonymous with breakfast, especially on board where toast and marmalade are just not good enough for a ravenous crew. In order for everyone to get off on the right foot for the day, the following classic recipes will ensure you don't fail as the breakfast cook.

Fried potatoes, bacon and sausages go extremely well with any of the egg recipes and should keep everyone happy for a few hours. However, if you are in a stormy situation or in heavy seas, then resort to the Rosti potatoes in your store cupboard, together with some scrambled eggs.

Fried Eggs

Heat some butter in a frying pan but do not allow it to become too hot or the eggs will become tough. Break in the desired number of eggs and cook over a moderate heat while basting with the fat. When the whites are set but the yolks are still soft, lift the eggs out with a slotted spatula.

Scrambled Eggs

These should be cooked very slowly, until soft, or set according to taste.

Beat the eggs, allowing one to two eggs per person depending on appetites. Whisk until thoroughly mixed and slightly frothy. Using a heavy based pan, melt half a tablespoon of butter per egg, and add the beaten eggs, cooking very slowly over a low heat, while stirring constantly with a wooden spatula. The eggs should start to thicken after three minutes. Continue cooking very slowly, scraping the cooked egg from the side and bottom of the pan. If they start to thicken too quickly, remove from the heat and cool a little before continuing to cook.

Just before they are ready, remove from the heat as the cooking process will continue with the heat of the pan. Stir in butter according to taste and serve at once.

Poached Eggs

Eggs for poaching must be very fresh.

Fill a saucepan two thirds full of water adding a tablespoon of vinegar. Bring to the boil. First dip each egg in its shell into the boiling water for about ten seconds then remove. Then break an egg into a bubbly patch and repeat the process, adding up to four eggs. Cook for approximately one and half minutes. The egg white should be firm and the yolk soft. Lift out the eggs with a slotted spoon.

Note: For the late risers on night watch, poached eggs can be kept for an hour or two in cold water, then drained. They can then be reheated by plunging them into boiling water for a few moments.

Boiled Eggs

There is a lot of controversy about how to cook a perfect boiled egg.
I tend to favour Mrs Beeton's recipe.

Ideally, eggs should be at room temperature. Bring a small saucepan of water to the boil, allowing enough water to cover the eggs. Place the eggs on a spoon and lower one at a time into the water. Begin timing the cooking as soon as the egg is in the water. Regulate the heat so the water stays just on the boil.

Average size eggs:
Soft boiled $3\frac{1}{4}$ minutes
Medium 4 - $3\frac{3}{4}$ minutes
Hard - 10 minutes

French Toast

Stale bread makes ideal French toast, if it is too fresh it will absorb too much of the egg mixture. It is particularly delicious when seasoned with some ground cinnamon, grated lemon or orange peel, or a few drops of vanilla essence.

Serves four

2 eggs
115ml/4fl oz milk
4 slices stale bread
Butter
Seasoning of your choice

Combine the eggs, milk and seasoning. Dip the bread into the egg mixture and cook on both sides in hot butter until golden.

Omelette

Serves one

Beat three eggs, seasoned with a pinch of salt and pepper, until the white and yolks are fully blended. Heat the omelette pan or skillet and add a tablespoon of butter. When the butter starts to foam, pour in the eggs. Immediately start sliding the pan back and forth at an angle, pulling the egg mixture in from the sides.

As the eggs become custard like on the bottom of the pan it is at this point you may add a filling if required. Lift the pan and run your fork or spoon around the edge of the omelette to make sure it is not sticking to the pan. Let the omelette curl over itself by shaking the pan on a steep angle, helping the edges with your fork. Then hold the pan over the heat for a few seconds to brown lightly. Serve.

Frittata with Onions and Sun Dried Tomatoes

Frittata is an open omelette, cooked very slowly, into which you can add a number of different vegetables and meats. These omelettes can be served hot or cold and make an ideal lunch dish.

Serves four

500g/1lb red onions, finely chopped
5 tablespoons of virgin olive oil
8 free range eggs
125g/4^1/$_2$ oz sun dried tomatoes in olive oil, drained and chopped
Salt and pepper

Heat the olive oil in a heavy bottomed frying pan. Add the onions and cook gently for about 30 minutes. Break the eggs into a bowl and beat lightly before adding the sun dried tomatoes and the cooked onions. Return the mixture to the frying pan, having added a little more oil. Cook gently, without stirring until it has set.

Place under a grill until the top has set. If you do not have a grill, then place in a preheated oven until set.

Mushroom Frittata

This is an ideal lunchtime menu. Most of the ingredients could be in your store locker.

Serves four

2 shallots or one red onion
1 clove of garlic peeled and chopped
3 tablespoons of extra virgin olive oil
225g/8oz assorted mushrooms depending on what is available
** (or dried)**
Juice of half a lemon
8 free range eggs
150ml/5fl oz double or whipping cream
15g/^{1}/2oz butter
Salt and pepper

Heat two tablespoons of olive oil in an ovenproof pan. Add the chopped shallots or red onions and the garlic and sauté until they are translucent. Add the mushrooms and lemon juice and stir occasionally before raising the heat to reduce the liquid. Put to one side.

Meanwhile beat the eggs and cream together and season with salt and pepper. Add the onion and mushroom mixture to the eggs. Heat one tablespoon of olive oil in the pan and pour in the combined mixture. Cook until the bottom of the frittata is just beginning to set. Place in the oven and leave for about 20 minutes until the top has just set.

Facing page: Spaghetti with Mussels (page 82).

PASTA

The versatility of pasta, so quick and easy to prepare as well as being economical, makes it a necessity aboard a boat. Other staples, such as potatoes, require careful storage and have a tendency to rot. Pasta, on the other hand, can have a shelf life of up to two years.

Pasta is also extremely nourishing and easily digested. It releases energy slowly over a long period of time and consequently is ideal for an evening meal before the long night watch. I have allowed an average of 112g/4oz of pasta per person which should be sufficient for those with hearty appetites.

Many of the ingredients for pasta dishes can be kept in your store locker – nine of the dishes in this chapter are store locker recipes.

With space such a premium aboard, I would not expect to store too many different types of pasta. I have suggested a type of pasta for each recipe but this can easily be changed without altering the dish significantly. So, before shopping for your store locker, decide which type of pasta would be the most useful to you.

Spaghetti with Lemon and Pine Nuts

Pine nuts are very useful to have aboard. However, their shelf life is not long, so check the sell-by date and make sure they are stored in a dry place.

Serves four to six

450g/1lb spaghetti
Juice of three lemons
150ml/6fl oz virgin olive oil
150g/5oz grated Parmesan
150g/5oz pine nuts
Salt and freshly ground pepper

Mix the lemon juice with the olive oil and Parmesan to a creamy sauce. Season with the salt and pepper. Roast the pine nuts gently in a frying pan until golden brown. Meanwhile, cook the pasta in a large pot of boiling water until *al dente*. Drain and add the sauce. Finally, add the pine nuts and a little grated lemon.

Spaghetti alla Carbonara

This is an old favourite which is easy to make and ideal for serving up when the crew are tired and hungry.

Serves four

450g/1lb spaghetti
225g/8oz bacon or pancetta chopped
3 egg yolks
220ml/8fl oz double or whipping cream
100g/3 1/2oz grated Parmesan cheese
1 tablespoon of olive oil
Salt and pepper

Heat a little olive oil in a large pan and sauté the bacon or pancetta until slightly brown.

Beat the eggs yolks and cream together and season with salt and pepper. Add the Parmesan. Meanwhile, cook the spaghetti in boiling water, and drain. Return to the pan, stir in the bacon or pancetta and the oil.

Pour in the cream mixture. Toss the spaghetti gently. The heat from the pasta will lightly cook the egg mixture. Return to the heat for a few seconds. Do not overcook.

Serve with grated Parmesan cheese.

Spaghetti Bolognese

This is probably one of the most loved and traditional of all the pasta dishes. If possible cook the sauce a day in advance. As with all stews, the flavours improve with time. It's always a good idea, if you have the time and space, to make double the quantity of sauce and freeze.

Serves four

450g/1lb spaghetti
450g/1lb minced beef
400g/14oz can tomatoes, chopped
3 tablespoons of olive oil
25g/1oz butter
1 onion, finely chopped
2 sticks of celery, finely chopped
2 cloves of garlic, chopped
50g/2oz prosciutto, or bacon, finely chopped
25g/1oz dried porcini mushrooms, soaked in warm water for
**   20 minutes, then drained**
1 glass red wine
140g/5oz can tomato purée
250ml/8fl oz beef or chicken stock
1 tablespoon dried mixed herbs
Salt and freshly ground black pepper
50g/2oz Parmesan cheese, grated

Heat the olive oil and butter and sauté the bacon or prosciutto until it starts to turn brown. Add the onions, celery and garlic. Gently sauté together until the onion is transparent. Add the minced beef and when the meat has browned, stir in the tomatoes, dried mixed herbs, tomato purée and the can of tomatoes. When the mixture is simmering, add the mushrooms, pour in the wine and stock. Bring back to the boil. Season with salt and freshly ground black pepper.

Cover and simmer gently for one hour before removing the lid and continue to cook for a further 20 minutes to reduce the liquid.

When the sauce is ready, cook the spaghetti in plenty of boiling, salted water until it is *al dente*. Pour the Bolognese sauce over it and serve with grated Parmesan cheese.

Spaghetti with Mussels

Serves four

450g/1lb spaghetti
4 dozen mussels cleaned
2 tablespoons of olive oil
4 shallots, finely chopped
2 cloves of garlic, peeled and chopped
2 tablespoons of parsley, chopped
2 sprigs of thyme
1 bay leaf
175ml/6oz dry white wine
400g/14oz can of tomatoes, chopped

In a frying pan sauté the finely chopped shallots and garlic in the oil until transparent. Add the dry white wine, parsley, thyme, bay leaf and pepper. Reduce for one minute then add the tomatoes. Simmer for ten minutes.

Heat half the olive oil in a large, heavy saucepan. Add the mussels, cover and cook briefly over a high heat until the mussels open. This should take about five minutes. Drain the mussels, keeping the liquid. When they are cool, remove them from their shells. Add the mussels and their liquid to the wine and tomatoes. Reheat gently.

Cook the spaghetti in boiling, salted water. Drain and add the sauce. If necessary add more olive oil.

Spaghetti with Virgin Olive Oil and Garlic

This is another simple pasta dish, a perfect dish to make when your store locker is low. All you need is spaghetti, olive oil, garlic and Parmesan.

Serves four

450g/1lb spaghetti
5 cloves of garlic, peeled and roughly crushed
175ml/6fl oz virgin olive oil
Salt and freshly ground black pepper
Parmesan cheese

Heat the olive oil in a heavy saucepan. Add the garlic and cook until it just starts to turn brown. Remove from the oil and discard.

Meanwhile, cook the spaghetti in a large saucepan of salted water until *al dente*. Drain and pour the oil over the spaghetti and toss gently with the Parmesan.

Season with salt and freshly ground black pepper.

Variation: If you favour your food a little hot and spicy – when cooking the garlic, add three dried chilli peppers to the olive oil and discard along with the garlic.

Serve with a green salad.

Fettucine with Walnut Sauce

Serves four

450g/1lb fettuccine
225g/8oz walnuts, shelled and pounded with a pestle and mortar
to a fine powder or ground in a blender. Keep a few chopped
walnuts aside for decoration.
1 slice white bread
250ml/8fl oz of milk
1 clove of garlic, crushed
3 tablespoons of olive oil (even better with walnut oil if available)
3 tablespoons of mascarpone cheese or cream cheese
100g/3 1/2oz grated Parmesan cheese
Salt and pepper

Soak the bread in the milk. Mix the powdered walnuts with the garlic. Squeeze the bread and add it to the powdered walnuts and garlic. Add the olive oil and while slowly stirring, add the mascarpone or cream cheese.

Cook the fettuccine in plenty of boiling, salted water, until *al dente*. Drain and return to the saucepan. Pour over the sauce and serve with the Parmesan cheese and the remaining chopped walnuts.

Fettucine with Pesto

This is a great favourite of mine. Make an extra amount of pesto and the sauce can be used in other recipes – try pesto sauce with grilled pork chops, it's delicious. The sauce can be made either with a pestle and mortar or with a blender.

Serves four

450g/1lb fettucine
1 large bunch fresh basil
2 large cloves of garlic, crushed
50g/2oz pine nuts
50g/2oz Parmesan cheese
2 tablespoons olive oil
175m/6fl oz double or whipping cream (optional)

Mix the basil leaves in a blender (or pound the leaves in a pestle and mortar). Add the pine nuts, garlic and the cheese and when all the ingredients have formed a thick paste, add the olive oil, a little at a time, making sure you blend it well in with the other ingredients.

If you have made double the quantity of sauce, store the remaining pesto in a jar, making sure it is covered with olive oil to preserve it. It should last up to three weeks in the fridge.

Cook the fettuccine until *al dente*. Drain, then add the cream and pesto sauce. Heat through gently and serve immediately with grated Parmesan cheese.

Fettuccine with Cream

This is another recipe which can be made with items from the store locker.

Serves four

450g/1lb fettuccine
50g/2oz butter
3 large eggs
175ml/6fl oz cream
100g/3¹/₂oz grated Parmesan cheese
Salt and pepper

Beat the eggs and cream in a bowl until well mixed. Season with salt and pepper. Cook the fettuccine in a lot of boiling, salted water, until *al dente*. Drain the fettuccine and pour the eggs and cream mixture over the top. Place over a low heat for a few seconds and toss so the pasta is well covered with the sauce. Be careful not to overcook.

Serve with fresh Parmesan cheese and season with salt and pepper.

Fettuccine with Gorgonzola or Roquefort Cheese

This is easy and quick to make as well as being a very tasty dish. The items could be in your fridge or store locker and could be made up at the last minute, when the storm has died down, or you have dropped anchor and everyone is starving hungry.

Serves four

450g/1lb fettuccine
150g/5oz Gorgonzola or Roquefort cheese (or any blue cheese)
  broken into pieces
175ml/6fl oz cream
25g/1oz melted butter
Salt and freshly ground black pepper

Cook the fettuccine in plenty of boiling, salted water, until *al dente*. Meanwhile combine the cheese and the cream in a pan and heat gently until all the ingredients have amalgamated. Do not allow it to boil.

Drain the fettuccine, then toss it in the melted butter. Add the sauce and place over a low heat for a few seconds. Season with salt and pepper.

Tagliatelle with Mushrooms

If fresh mushrooms are not available, this recipe can be made from a combination of the dried and canned variety in your store locker.

Serves four

420g/14oz tagliatelle
25g/1oz dried porcini
150ml/6oz hot water
450g/1lb fresh or canned mushrooms
50g/2oz melted butter
2 tablespoons olive oil
2 cloves of garlic, peeled and chopped
1 handful of parsley, chopped
425ml/15oz double or whipping cream
Salt and freshly ground black pepper

Soak the porcini in hot water for 20 minutes. Wipe the mushrooms and slice lengthways. Heat the oil and butter together in a frying pan and sauté the garlic and parsley gently. Do not allow to brown. Add the porcini and mushrooms and cook over a high heat for a few minutes.

Cook the tagliatelle in boiling, salted water until *al dente*. Drain. Add the cream to the tagliatelle and heat gently. Add the porcini and mushrooms and toss gently. Season with salt and freshly ground pepper and Parmesan cheese.

Capelli D'Angelo (Angel's Hair Pasta) with Asparagus

You can use either fresh or canned asparagus for this simple to make dish, although fresh is obviously tastier.

Serves four

500g/1lb 1oz fresh or canned asparagus
450g/1lb capelli d'angelo pasta
100g/3 1/2 oz unsalted butter
1 tablespoon parsley
150ml/5fl oz cream (long life cream if you haven't any fresh)
100g/3 1/2 oz grated Parmesan
Salt and freshly ground black pepper

Scrape the thick stalks of the asparagus and tie into a bundle before placing (preferably upright) in a pan of rapidly boiling water. Boil for ten minutes or until tender. Drain the asparagus but keep the water. Cut off the spear ends. If using the canned version, drain the asparagus and retain the water.

Melt the butter in a frying pan, add the garlic and parsley. Meanwhile add the asparagus water to the pasta cooking water and bring to the boil before adding the capelli d'angelo.

Add the asparagus spears to the garlic, parsley and cream. Simmer for a few minutes but do not allow the mixture to boil. Season. Drain the pasta and pour the sauce over it. Add the Parmesan and toss gently.

Conchiglie with Broccoli and Spring Onions

The delicate flavour of the broccoli compares favourably with the stronger taste of the spring onions in this simple, easy to make dish.

Serves four

450g/1lb conchiglie (shells)
350g/12oz broccoli florets
8 spring onions, finely chopped
120g/4oz butter
75g/3oz Parmesan cheese, shaved (use a vegetable peeler)
Salt and freshly ground black pepper

Melt the butter in an earthenware dish, add the spring onions and lightly cook for two minutes. Cook the broccoli florets in boiling water, drain and put to one side. Keep warm.

Meanwhile, cook the conchiglie in a large quantity of boiling, salted water until *al dente*. Drain, then add to the earthenware dish with the melted butter and spring onion. Season with salt and pepper, toss gently and add the broccoli. Serve immediately with shaved Parmesan cheese.

Tip: To keep vegetables warm when they have been strained, put back into the pan and cover with a paper towel until ready to serve.

Farfalle with Tomato and Pancetta Sauce

This is a good standby when stores are running low. The pancetta may be replaced by bacon.

450g/1lb farfalle pasta (or any other pasta in your store locker)
1 tablespoon dried mixed herbs
1 onion, finely chopped
2 cloves garlic, chopped
100g/3^{1}/2oz pancetta or bacon, finely chopped
800g/1lb 12oz canned tomatoes, chopped
Salt and freshly ground black pepper

In a large frying pan sauté the pancetta or bacon with the onion and garlic until the onion is transparent. Add the tomatoes, season with the salt, pepper and herbs and simmer for about 30 minutes. Cook the farfalle in plenty of boiling, salted water. Drain and pour the sauce over the pasta.

Tortiglioni with Tomatoes

If you happen to be in port try to buy some fresh herbs such as basil, chives and parsley. If these are not available, use dried mixed herbs.

Serves four

450g/1lb tortiglioni
800g/1lb 12oz (or two 14oz) tins tomatoes, chopped
175g/6oz sun dried tomatoes, chopped
3 tablespoons of olive oil
2 cloves garlic, chopped
2 handfuls fresh basil, chopped (or 1 teaspoon dried mixed herbs)
100g/3¹/2oz grated Parmesan cheese
Salt and freshly ground black pepper

Heat the olive oil in a saucepan and sauté the garlic until golden brown. Add the tomatoes and herbs. Simmer gently for about 30 minutes then add the sun dried tomatoes, return to the heat for a further five minutes. Season with salt and pepper.

Cook the pasta in plenty of boiling, salted water. Drain and put into a serving bowl before adding the tomato sauce and the Parmesan cheese.

Serve immediately.

Facing page: Fish Market, Mahon, Menorca.

FISH
AND FISHING

A short word about fishing for the uninitiated. Our fishing experience was non-existent until a friend enlightened our son Rohan. Eventually Captain John decided that perhaps he would allow a fishing line onboard, especially in the light of an imminent crossing during which we would not be seeing land, let alone having the opportunity for any shopping, for some time.

We have never looked back. We cruised from Menorca to Gibraltar and, in our four days at sea, caught at least one tuna per day. We ate raw fish Japanese style: Sashimi with Ginger and Wasabi. After one mouthful we were all convinced that this was the only way to eat freshly caught tuna. Looking back on the experience and popping into the local fishmonger, I am unnerved at the price of fresh fish and how extravagant we were. But it was one of the high spots of that trip.

Suggested fishing gear

A rod and a good reel, with 100lb test line and a rod holder attached to the rail. Alternatively, you could use a 100lb test line with a bungie set up. Other items in your fishing tackle box could include: a teaser, box of swivels, stainless hooks, stainless wire, green, blue and pink plastic squid lures, and some silver spoon lures.

Make sure you have a gaff with a long enough handle to reach the water and pull out the fish. A pair of heavy-duty garden gloves always comes in useful, as does a good filleting knife.

A few fishing tips

Don't put out too much line. The lure should be about 100 feet away, or just at the end of the turbulence caused by the wake of your boat. The best time to fish is when the sea is agitated, and your sailing speed about five to six knots. This is not necessarily the easiest time to pull in a fish, but it is when you are most likely to catch them. Once the fish is on board, the most humane way of killing it is to pour cheap alcohol into the gills. Keep a watch out for seagulls flying close and diving into the water. They are feeding on small fish and bigger fry will be underneath, so you may consider changing course to follow the birds.

One word of warning: If you are fishing in the Caribbean beware of catching fish found in the reef areas, such as barracuda or snapper. They may be poisonous with the toxin ciguatera, which attacks the nervous system when eaten. As a general rule only eat fish smaller than five pounds to limit the risk. If the fish won't fit on your plate, don't eat it.

Fish and Shellfish

Fish and shellfish exist in an amazing variety – in European waters alone there are over a hundred species. Most of the recipes included in this chapter list one or more substitutes for the fish specified.

Here are a few general points if you have to buy fish. Firstly, do not buy fish on a Monday. It's likely to have been caught on the previous Friday. The fish should be shiny, the eyes should be bright with black pupils and transparent corneas.

Fresh fish should not have a fishy smell. Do not keep the fish more than two days. If you are thinking of keeping it longer, you should freeze it. Whole fish also keeps better than filleted fish, so bear this in mind when purchasing before a trip, making sure that if you are freezing the fish, it is very fresh and no more than a day or so old.

If you are lucky enough to catch your own fish, gut it immediately. Shellfish deteriorate more rapidly than fish. Seafood will not keep longer than one day if stored in the fridge. Wrap loosely in a plastic bag or aluminium foil to prevent the smell penetrating other foods.

The majority of the recipes contained in this chapter involve baking as this is more suitable for life afloat. However, there are a number of other recipes in the chapter on barbecuing, included later in this book. Barbecuing is unsurpassed as a method of bringing out the best flavour in freshly caught fish.

Cleaning and Gutting Fish – The Essential Steps

It is unlikely that you would buy fish ungutted, but if you have been lucky enough to catch a fish, here are a few tips:

First trim off the fins with a pair of scissors. Then scale the fish, using the edge of a knife and making sure to scrape towards the head from the tail.

Scale the fish in the sink, with some water, to avoid scales flying around the galley.

Once you have removed the scales, slit the belly from the anal fin to the head and scrape out the guts. If the head has to be removed, cut off the head from the last gill. Make sure that you wash the cavity well, removing all blood.

If you need to gut a fish in such a way as to be able to stuff it whole, cut away the gills, then pull out the insides with your fingers. Make a small incision in front of the anal fin and then rinse through the gills with water.

Squid: only the tentacles and body sac are eaten. All the other parts are discarded. Clean the squid by holding the sac with one hand while pulling the head and tentacles with the other. Cut off the tentacles from the head, just in front of the eyes. There is a tiny hard lump at the top of the tentacle. Squeeze this out and throw it away. Keep the tentacles. Reach into the sac and remove the rest of the insides, including the long flexible plastic-like quill. Rinse running water through the sac and remove anything remaining.

To make your life easier once you have chosen a recipe, I have grouped the fish into categories in case you cannot find the appropriate fish for a given dish. They all make good substitutes for each other.

The following **white fish** are highly versatile:

Bass	Hake	Mullet	Cod
Bream	Monkfish	Whiting	Haddock

Flat fish are simple and a joy to cook and they are also easy to fillet. My favourite out of this group is turbot, which has an incredible flavour:

Brill	Flounder	Skate	Turbot
Halibut	Plaice	Sole	

Oily fish are perhaps not the best fish to have on board, unless you have caught them fresh, as they deteriorate quickly. However, they cook well on the barbecue or under the grill.

Anchovies	Herring	Mackerel	Sardines	Tuna

Fish

There can be few things more frustrating than to find yourself in a Mediterranean fish market, but unable to identify the bewildering varieties of fish on offer. Here are just a few of the fish available in fishmarkets throughout the Mediterranean and Atlantic shores and hopefully the translations will help you if your Italian, Spanish or French is not up to score.

English	French	Spanish	Italian
Anchovy	Anchois	Anchoa	Acciuga
Atlantic Salmon	Saumon d'atlantique	Salmón	Salmone
Barracuda	Barracuda	Espetón	Barracuda
Blue fin Tuna	Thon	Atun/bonito	Tonno
Brill	Barbue	Rémol	Rombo Liscio
Cod	Morue	Bacalao	Merluzzo
Dolphin Fish	Dorade tropicale	Lampuga	Lampuga
Flounder	Flet	Platija/platusa	Passera
Haddock	Aiglefin	Eglefino	Eglefino
Hake	Merlu/Colin	Merluza	Nasello
Halibut	Flétan	Fletán	Halibut
Herring	Hareng	Arenque	Aringa
Mackerel	Maquereau	Caballa	Sgombro
Monkfish	Baudroie	Rape	Rana Pescatrice
Plaice	Plie/Carrelet	Platija/solla	Platessa
Red Mullet	Rouget	Salmonete	Triglia
Sardine	Sardine	Sardina	Sardina
Sea Bass	Bar	Lubina	Spigola
Sea Bream	Brème	Pargo	Orata
Skate	Raie	Raya	Razza
Sole	Sole	Lenguado	Sogliola
Sword Fish	Espadon	Pez Espada	Pesce Spada
Trout	Truite	Trucha	Trota
Turbot	Turbot	Rodaballo	Rombo Chiodato
Whiting	Merlan	Merlán/plegonero	Merlano

Shellfish

English	French	Spanish	Italian
Blue Crab	Crabe Bleu	Cangrejo Azul	Granchio
Clam	Palourde	Almeja	Vongola
Cuttlefish	Seiche	Sepia/Jibia	Seppia
Dublin Bay Prawn	Langoustine	Langostino	Scampo
European Lobster	Homard	Langosta	Aragosta
European Oyster	Huitre	Bogavante	Ostrica
Med. Scallop	Coquille St Jacques	Vieira	Canestrello
Mussel	Moule	Mejillón	Cozza
Octopus	Pieuvre	Pulpo	Polpo
Prawn	Crevette	Gamba	Gambero
Shrimp	Crevette	Camarón	Gamberetto
Squid	Calmar	Calamar	Calamaro

The word 'prawn' covers a vast variety of shellfish, and can be confusing. For instance the Dublin Bay prawn (langoustine in French and langostino in Spanish) is a member of the lobster family, as are Danish lobster and Italian scampi.

Facing page: Rohan, aged 12, with freshly caught mahi mahi.

Squid with Garlic

This is a good lunchtime menu, served with salad and hot bread.

Serves four

4 medium sized squid
8 cloves of garlic, peeled and chopped
2 tablespoons of white wine
2 tablespoons of virgin olive oil
2 tablespoons of chopped parsley

Preheat the oven to 220°C/425°F/Gas Mark 7

Mix all the ingredients together, except the chopped parsley and squid. Place the squid in an ovenproof shallow dish and pour over the ingredients. Bake for twenty minutes.

Sprinkle with the chopped parsley and serve with salad and hot bread.

Red Mullet or Sea Bass cooked in Wine, Parsley and Garlic

Serves four

This could be served as a light lunch dish with salad and fresh bread, or for a more substantial meal, with mashed potatoes.

8 small red mullet, gutted
1 tablespoon of chopped parsley
4 tablespoons of olive oil
500ml/18fl oz of white wine

Preheat oven to 230°C/450°F/Gas Mark 8

Place the gutted mullet in an ovenproof dish. In a frying pan cook the parsley and garlic in the olive oil, until slightly brown. Allow to cool before pouring over the fish along with the white wine. Put in the preheated oven and cook for ten minutes.

Serve immediately.

Mati's Shrimp with Linguine

This delicious Spanish recipe, which is so quick and easy to make, was passed on to me by a sailing friend, Mati. Whenever I see shrimps in the market I cannot avoid buying them to make this marvellous, simple dish.

Serves four

450g/1lb linguine
60ml/2fl oz olive oil
625g/1¹/₄lbs of peeled shrimps
4 cloves of garlic, chopped
2 tablespoons of parsley, chopped
60ml/2fl oz lemon juice

Boil the linguine in a large saucepan of salted boiling water for about 8-10 minutes, until it is *al dente*.

Five minutes before the linguine is ready, heat the olive oil in a heavy bottomed pan and sauté the garlic and parsley. Add the shrimp and cook them for about a minute. Turn the shrimp over and cook for a short while until pink, then add the lemon juice cook for a few more seconds.
Drain the linguine and pour over the sauce. Toss, adding more olive oil if necessary. Serve immediately.

Baked Red/Black Bream or Daurade

If none of the above are available you could also use any of the following: red or grey mullet, sea bass.

Serves four

Bream weighing about 2kg/4 1/2lb in total, gutted and cleaned
3 fennel bulbs, chopped
1 red onion, peeled and chopped
2 bay leaves, crushed
3 cloves of garlic, peeled and chopped
1 glass of white wine
Dried mixed herbs
Juice of 1/2 lemon
50ml/2fl oz of virgin olive oil
Aluminium foil

Preheat the oven to 200°C/400°F/Gas Mark 6

Heat the olive oil in a frying pan and gently cook all the ingredients, except the fish, until the fennel is soft.

Make several diagonal incisions on both sides of the fish, right down to the bone. Season with salt and pepper, and place a tablespoon of the above mixture in the cavity of the fish. Put half of the remaining mixture on the bottom of an ovenproof dish, place the fish on top and cover it with the rest of the mixture. Then cover the dish with foil and bake for twenty minutes or until the fish is cooked.

Serve with boiled potatoes.

Baked Hake with Potatoes and Onions

If hake is unavailable, then you could use cod or haddock.

Serves four

850g/1¾lbs of fish fillets
3 large potatoes, sliced
2 onions, finely sliced
400g/14oz can of tomatoes, chopped
1 glass of white wine
220ml/8fl oz of virgin olive oil

Preheat the oven to 200°C/400°F/Gas Mark 6

Oil the bottom of an ovenproof dish and layer the potatoes alternatively with the sliced onions. Lay the fish fillets on top, cover with the chopped tomatoes. Season with salt and pepper and add the olive oil. Bake in the preheated oven for 15 minutes, then lower the temperature to 170°C/325°F or Gas Mark 3 and cook for 30 minutes. Then add the white wine and return to the oven for a further 15 minutes.

Baked Sea Bass en Papillote

I'm convinced this is one of the best methods for cooking fish because the essential flavours and aromas are retained in the parcel. Most types of fish may be cooked in this manner and you can vary the flavours by adding different fresh herbs and other ingredients.

Serves four

1 x 2.5kg/6lb sea bass, cleaned and filleted
110g/4oz of mushrooms, chopped
Few sprigs of fresh or dried thyme
Virgin olive oil
110g/4oz of butter
Aluminium foil

Preheat the oven to 200°C/400°F/Gas Mark 6

Fry the mushrooms gently in a little olive oil for a few minutes.

Make four rectangles of foil, brush with oil and place a fillet in the middle of each rectangle, skin side down. Cover with a few mushrooms, sprigs of thyme and a knob of butter. Season with salt and pepper. Seal the edges making a loose airtight package. Place the packages on a baking tray and bake in the oven for approximately ten minutes.

If you do not have any fresh mushrooms, you could use dried porcini mushrooms, which should be soaked in hot water for 20 minutes, then drained prior to use.

Ceviche

This is a marvellous South American dish, which works anywhere, and is a delightful first course. Halibut, salmon, tuna, monkfish, or brill can be used.

Serves four

450g/1lb of filleted fish cut into thin slices
Juice of 4 limes
1 red onion, thinly sliced
1 tablespoon of virgin olive oil
Cayenne pepper
1 fresh or dried chilli pepper, deseeded and chopped

Place the filleted fish onto a shallow serving dish. Mix all the other ingredients together, and cover the fillets with the mixture. Leave in a cool place for approximately six hours. Some varieties of fish may not need so long.

The fish is ready when it is opaque white. Season with salt and pepper and serve with avocado and salsa. See recipe on page 136.

Moules à la Marinière

This recipe is one of the tastiest ways to enjoy mussels. As most ports sell fresh mussels, this recipe is a must for anyone living aboard a boat.

Serves four

2kgs/4¹/2lbs mussels scrubbed, with all 'beards' removed
4 shallots, finely chopped
3 tablespoons chopped parsley
2 tablespoons butter
400ml/³/4pint dry white wine
2 sprigs of thyme
1 bayleaf

Beurre Manié
made by creaming together:
2 tablespoons of butter
1 tablespoon of flour

In a large saucepan, sauté the chopped shallots in 2 tablespoons of butter until transparent, then add the parsley, white wine, thyme and bay leaf. Season with salt and pepper. Simmer for ten minutes.

Add the mussels to the liquid, cover and cook over a high heat for a few minutes, shaking the pan constantly until all the shells are open. Discard any mussels that haven't opened. Transfer the mussels to a heated serving dish and keep warm. Over a high heat reduce the liquid to half its original quantity and thicken by adding the beurre manié. Whisk in the lemon juice and pour the sauce over the mussels.

Serve immediately.

Tuna Steaks with Red Onions and Balsamic Vinegar

Serves four

700g/1lb 8oz of tuna steak, cut into four portions
1kg/2lbs red onions
2 tablespoons virgin olive oil
2 tablespoons balsamic vinegar
3 cloves of garlic, peeled and chopped
Salt and pepper

Sauté the onions in a heavy casserole for 20 minutes and then proceed to caramelise them by turning up the heat. Add the garlic and balsamic vinegar, salt and pepper. Remove from casserole and put to one side.

Place the steaks in the casserole. Pour over the onions, garlic and balsamic vinegar and cover with aluminium foil.

Put the lid on the casserole and cook gently for fifteen minutes turning the steaks over half-way through cooking.

Serve with rice.

Facing page: Duck with Orange Glaze (page 132).

MEAT
AND POULTRY

Casseroles, Pot Roasts and Braised Dishes

The following recipes are ideal for cooking aboard. Casseroles have the advantage of being very flexible, they can be cooked in advance, frozen, or left simmering during a sail change. Nothing can be more welcoming or comforting than the warm, savoury smell of a casserole that has been simmering gently for several hours. The meat will melt in the mouth, and the vegetables, herbs and stock will have fused and blended their flavours. I have often made the mistake of leaving the remains of a casserole on the stove to cool overnight, only to find it had disappeared by the morning, devoured by the crew who were on the night watch. Pot roasts are equally useful, easy to prepare and always very tasty.

Boeuf à la Bourguignonne

This is one of the greatest of all traditional French beef dishes. It can be prepared well in advance – the flavour actually improves if it is cooked a day ahead.

Serves six

225g/8oz of bacon, cut into lardons (small strips)
1 tablespoon of olive oil
1kg/350g/3lbs lean stewing beef, cut into 2.5cm/1 inch squares
1 medium size onion, sliced
1 carrot, sliced
2 tablespoons of flour
425ml/3/4 pint of red wine
275ml/1/2 pint of beef stock
1 tablespoon of tomato paste
2 cloves of garlic, crushed
12 small white onions (if available)
225g/8oz of fresh mushrooms
Salt and freshly ground pepper

Preheat the oven to 170°C/325°F/Gas Mark 3

Heat the oil in a heavy flameproof casserole and sauté the bacon strips. When the bacon becomes brown remove it with a slotted spoon. Then sauté the sliced onion and carrots until translucent. Add the meat and cook until brown before returning the cooked bacon to the pan.

Sprinkle with flour seasoned with salt and pepper. Stir to soak up all the juices and cook for several minutes before adding the garlic, herbs and the tomato paste. Gradually stir in the wine and enough stock to cover the meat. Bring to the boil, then cover and cook in the oven or on top of the stove for at least two hours.

While the meat is cooking, prepare the remaining vegetables. Peel the small white onions and sauté them gently for a few minutes. Slice the mushrooms.

After two hours add the onions and mushrooms and simmer for a further hour or until the meat is tender.

Serve with boiled potatoes, noodles or steamed rice.

Veau Poêle
(Pot Roasted Veal)

This is a very simple but tasty dish cooked on top of the stove.

Serves six

1kg.350g/3lbs veal joint
2 tablespoons olive oil
2 carrots, chopped
2 sliced onions (red, if possible)
1 stick of celery, chopped
2 cloves of garlic, chopped
1 bouquet garni
Salt and freshly ground pepper

Heat the oil in a heavy flameproof casserole dish and brown the veal lightly. Remove the meat from the casserole. If the oil has burnt replace it with fresh oil before stirring in the carrots, onions, celery and garlic. Cook over a low heat for a few minutes until the onions are translucent. Return the veal to the casserole and lay it on top of the vegetables. Season with salt and pepper.

Place a layer of foil directly on top of the meat and vegetables and cover the dish with a tight fitting lid. Regulate the heat so the meat cooks slowly for about one and a half hours, basting from time to time. Prick the roast with a fork, it's ready when the juices run clear.

Remove the roast from the casserole and keep warm. Remove the excess fat from the juice in the casserole, and mash the vegetables with the juice from the meat.

Correct the seasoning and serve the juice and vegetables as a sauce for the meat, along with mashed potatoes and a green vegetable.

Blanquette de Veau
(Veal Stew with Onions and Mushrooms)

Many a comment has been made when I serve this delicious dish on *Jupiter Moon*. People ask how could I possibly cook Blanquette de Veau out at sea? In fact it is a great recipe to make when you have time, although I would suggest that you do not attempt to cook this in rough conditions. However, it is not a difficult recipe, and may be cooked in advance except for adding the cream and egg yolks at the end when you are ready to serve.

Serves six

1kg.350g/3lbs of stewing veal cut into 5cm/2 inch pieces
1 1/2 litres/3pts cold chicken stock
12 small onions (or 3 medium onions, chopped)
2 tablespoons butter
1 tablespoon of flour
12 button mushrooms (if unavailable, any type of mushrooms will do)
4 egg yolks
Juice of one lemon
150ml/1/4 pint double or whipping cream
Salt and freshly ground pepper

Heat the butter in a flameproof casserole and sauté the veal with the onions until the onions are golden. Sprinkle in the flour seasoned with salt and pepper. Stir and then add enough stock to cover the meat. Bring it slowly to simmering point and add a bouquet garni. Cover and simmer very slowly for about 45 minutes, then add the button mushrooms. Return to the heat and continue cooking for another half an hour, or until the meat is tender. When the meat is tender remove it from the casserole and keep warm.

To thicken the sauce: whisk the egg yolks, cream and lemon juice together in a bowl. Slowly beat in a ladle of the sauce from the veal. Pour this mixture back into the casserole dish containing the sauce and stir well. Return the meat to the sauce and heat through gently being careful not to let it boil or you risk curdling the cream.

Serve with rice, noodles or potatoes.

* This menu may be frozen, but add the yolks and cream mixture after defrosting.

Pork Stew with Lemon and Garlic

This recipe is admittedly a bit of a fiddle for on board cooking, but if you have a calm sea or are in port it is a lovely dish that does not take too long to cook.

Serves four

1kg/2lbs of pork tenderloin, cut into 5cm/2 inch cubes
Zest of half a lemon
2 cloves of garlic, chopped
25g/1oz prosciutto, finely chopped

Mix the lemon, garlic and prosciutto together. Make a hole in each of the cubes of meat and insert some of the mixture into each of the holes.

150g/5oz prosciutto, finely chopped
2 tablespoons olive oil
1 onion, peeled and chopped
1 carrot, peeled and chopped
1 stick of celery, chopped
1 glass of red wine
400g/14oz can tomatoes, chopped
1 litre of vegetable or chicken stock
Salt and freshly ground pepper

Heat the oil in a flameproof casserole and sauté the onions, prosciutto, carrot and celery together for five minutes. Add the meat to the casserole and gently brown on all sides. Pour in the wine and let it reduce for five minutes. Add the tomatoes and the meat stock, season with salt and pepper and simmer on top of the stove for about an hour or until the meat is tender.

Serve with mashed potatoes or with noodles.

Rôti de porc
(Casserole roasted pork)

This recipe requires a boneless joint of pork, loin is probably the best. As with pot roasted veal, if you baste the joint occasionally it will stay lovely and moist. And, of course, slow cooking will tenderise the meat so that it ends up melting in the mouth.

Serves four to six

1 1/2kg/3lb loin of pork joint
4 tablespoons of olive oil
2 tablespoons of butter
2 medium onions, peeled and sliced
1 carrot, sliced
2 cloves of garlic, unpeeled
1 bouquet garni
1 glass of dry white wine
150ml/1/4 pint of vegetable or chicken stock
Salt and freshly ground pepper

Preheat the oven to 160°C/325°F/Gas Mark 3

Heat the oil in a heavy, flameproof casserole and brown the pork joint on all sides. Put the meat to one side and discard the fat from the casserole dish. Add the butter, stir in the vegetables and cook for five minutes. Return the meat to the casserole, placing it on top of the vegetables. Season and then cover the meat and vegetables with foil and put on the lid. Place in the middle of the preheated oven, or on top of the stove. Baste from time to time. Cooking should take about two hours.

When the meat is cooked (i.e. when pierced with a knife the juice runs clear), put the joint aside and keep warm. Remove the excess fat from the casserole, add the wine and stock and mash the vegetables into the juice. Boil rapidly until you have reduced the liquid to about a cupful.

Serve with the pork.

Beef Braised in Beer with White Beans and Mushrooms

A hearty stew - try to prepare this in advance to make it even tastier.

Serves four

1kg/2lb 4oz braising steak cut into 5cm/2 inch cubes
250g/9oz cannellini beans, soaked overnight.
2 medium onions, sliced
4 tablespoons of olive oil
1 tablespoon of flour
350g/12oz mushrooms, sliced.
3 cloves of garlic
Sprigs of fresh thyme (if not available, a teaspoon of dried thyme will do)
570ml/1 pt beef stock
440ml/14oz can of stout
Salt and freshly ground pepper

Preheat the oven to 150°C/300°F/Gas Mark 2

Dust the meat with the flour which has been seasoned with salt and pepper. Heat 2 tablespoons of the olive oil in a frying pan and brown the meat. Put aside. Heat the remaining 2 tablespoons of olive oil in a heavy flameproof casserole, add the onions and cook until slightly brown. Add the meat to the onions. Drain the beans and add them to the meat and onions, along with the garlic and sprigs of thyme. Pour over the beef stock and the beer and bring to simmering point. Cover with a lid and place in the oven for two hours. Then add the mushrooms and cook for a further hour.

Serve with rice or potatoes.

Hungarian Goulash

Another easy recipe that can simmer away until you are ready to eat. Delicious served with mashed potatoes or noodles, this meal will give you plenty of energy until the early hours of the morning.

Serves six

900g/2lbs stewing steak or veal cut into 5cm/2 inch pieces
1 tablespoon of flour
2 onions, finely chopped
2 tablespoons of olive oil
2 tablespoons of paprika
1/2 teaspoon of caraway seeds
1 tablespoon of tomato paste
1 clove of garlic, crushed
400g/14oz can of chopped tomatoes
Salt and freshly ground pepper

Preheat the oven to 170°C/325°F/Gas Mark 3

Heat the oil in a heavy flameproof casserole and sauté the onions and garlic until transparent. Dust the meat with the flour seasoned with salt and pepper. Add the meat to the casserole and sauté until brown on all sides. Sprinkle with the paprika and caraway seeds, then add the tomato paste. Give the mixture a good stir before adding the chopped tomatoes and the beef stock, making sure the meat is covered with the liquid. Cover with a tight fitting lid and place in the oven for 2½ hours, or until the meat is tender.

This may also be cooked on top of the stove.

Fabada Asturiana

Fabada is a famous dish from Asturia in Northern Spain and the essential ingredient is beans. Originally these were broad beans but dried butter beans or broad beans may be used. The important thing is that the beans should not be too old, so check their sell-by-date.

Serves four to six

750g/1 1/2lbs beans, soaked in water overnight
250g/8oz bacon, chopped
250g/8oz salted pork belly, sliced
2 cloves of garlic, crushed
Pinch of saffron
175g/6oz black pudding or sausage, sliced thickly
175g/6oz chorizo sausage
Salt and freshly ground pepper

Drain the beans and put them in a heavy casserole with all the ingredients except the saffron and black pudding. Pour over enough water to cover everything and bring to the boil. Partially cover with a lid and simmer for one hour removing any scum from time to time. Meanwhile soak the saffron threads with a little boiling water, mash them and add to the casserole. Continue to simmer gently for 1 1/2-2 hours or until the beans are quite soft and the meat is tender. About ten minutes before the end add the black pudding and seasoning. If there is too much liquid remaining, remove the casserole lid, turn up the heat and boil rapidly to reduce the sauce.

Like many casseroles this dish will taste even better if cooked the day before.

Pork Braised in Balsamic Vinegar and Red Wine

This recipe, together with Lamb Braised in Red Wine and Balsamic Vinegar, have been adapted for galley cooking. They originally come from Ruth Rogers and Rose Gray, who have that marvellous restaurant, The River Café, in London.

Serves four

1kg/2lb tenderloin of pork
1 tablespoon of olive oil
2 red onions sliced
110g/4oz butter
1 tablespoon rosemary
275ml/1/2 pint balsamic vinegar
275ml/1/2 pint red wine
Salt and freshly ground pepper

Preheat the oven to 220°C/425°F/Gas Mark 7

Heat the oil in a frying pan and brown the pork on all sides at a high temperature. Put to one side. Heat the butter in a heavy flameproof casserole and sauté the onions and rosemary. Pour in the balsamic vinegar and the wine and reduce for five minutes. Then add the pork, making sure it has been well coated. Season and cook in the preheated oven for approximately 40 minutes, turning the pork from time to time. If it becomes too dry add more balsamic vinegar.
   When the pork is ready, slice and serve with the juice.

Serve with mashed potatoes or rice.

Lamb Braised in Red Wine and Balsamic Vinegar

If you can find lamb shanks so much the better. Unfortunately they are not always readily available, so buy shoulder of lamb with the fat removed and cut into bite-size pieces.

Serves four

4 lamb shanks or 1kg/2lb shoulder of lamb cut into bite size pieces
4 red onions, sliced
3 sprigs of fresh rosemary
2 tablespoons of olive oil
1 tablespoon of flour, seasoned with salt and freshly ground pepper
3 cloves of garlic, peeled and chopped
150ml/5fl oz balsamic vinegar
300ml/10fl oz red wine

Preheat the oven to 200°C/400°F/Gas Mark 6

Heat the oil in a heavy-bottomed casserole. Dust the lamb shanks or shoulder of lamb with the seasoned flour and brown the lamb. Remove the lamb, and the oil if it has burnt, putting the meat to one side. Replace the oil if necessary and add the onions. Sauté until light brown before adding the chopped rosemary and garlic. Cook for a few minutes. Pour in the red wine and balsamic vinegar and reduce the liquid over a high heat for a further five minutes before adding the lamb.
Cook in the oven for about 2 hours, checking the meat from time to time and adding more wine if it becomes too dry.

If you are cooking with shoulder of lamb then reduce the cooking time to 1½ hours.

Lamb Steaks Marinated in Oil and Lemon Juice

This is a quick and simple dish to make and can also be cooked on the barbecue. When you are marinating the lamb you can prepare the vegetables. Roasted vegetables would make a good accompaniment to this dish.

Serves four

4 lamb steaks
Juice of one lemon
2 tablespoons virgin olive oil
Sprig of fresh rosemary, chopped (or dried if fresh not available)
Salt and freshly ground pepper

Place the lamb steaks in an earthenware dish (always use a non-reactive metal or earthenware dish when marinating). Pour the lemon juice and olive oil over the lamb steaks, then sprinkle with the rosemary. Season with salt and pepper and leave to marinate for twenty minutes or longer, turning from time to time. Heat the grill to a medium/high temperature and cook the steaks for four minutes on each side.

Serve with oven roasted vegetables.

Osso Bucco Milanese

This is one of my favourite dishes. Preparation is easy and the result is delicious. However, in some parts of Europe, particularly in Spain, it is difficult to buy veal, but the beef there is very young and the cut is still called Osso Bucco, although you may have to cook it for a while longer.

Serves four

1kg/2lbs shin of veal cut in slices 5cm/2 inch thick
150ml/^{1}/4 pint white wine
150ml/^{1}/4 pint stock
400ml/14oz can of chopped tomatoes
50g/2oz butter
Salt and freshly ground pepper

Gremolata
1 clove of garlic, peeled and chopped
1 handful of chopped parsley
Zest of half lemon, finely chopped

Heat the butter in a flameproof casserole and brown the slices of veal. Arrange the meat in the bottom of the casserole, pour over the wine and let it reduce for about ten minutes. Add the chopped tomatoes and the stock and season with salt and pepper. Cover for the first hour, then take the lid off and continue cooking for another hour.

To make the gremolata, which traditionally accompanies this dish, mix the parsley, chopped garlic and lemon zest together and sprinkle on top of each piece of osso bucco before serving.

This dish is traditionally served with Risotto alla Milanese but unfortunately this is not always possible when at sea as the rice has to be watched and stirred frequently with the liquid added in stages. If you think risotto is too difficult to make due to your sailing conditions, substitute plain rice or try the quick cook Gallo risotto rice available from good delicatessens.

Gigot d'Agneau à la Moutarde
(Roast Lamb in a Mustard Sauce)

This recipe is easy and the results are delicious. Try to cover the lamb with the mixture a few hours before roasting, as this will enhance the flavour. Serve with new potoatoes and green beans.

Serves four to six

3kg/6lb leg of lamb

For the mixture
3 tablespoons Dijon mustard
2 tablespoons soy sauce
2 cloves of garlic, peeled and crushed
1 tablespoon of dried mixed herbs
2 tablespoons of honey
2 tablespoons of olive oil
Salt and freshly ground pepper

Preheat the oven to 180°C/350°F/Gas Mark 4

Blend all the ingredients for the mixture together except the olive oil. Slowly add drops of the olive oil, beating continously with a whisk, until it resembles a cream-like mixture. Paint the lamb with the mixture and put the lamb in the roasting pan.

Roast for 1 1/4 hours for medium rare, or 1 1/2 hours for well done.

Sauté de Boeuf
(Beef Sautéed with Cream and Mushrooms)

This is a marvellously quick dish which can be prepared and on the table within 30 minutes. However, make sure that you buy good quality beef.

Serves four

1kg/2lbs fillet of beef, cut into 1cm/^{1}/2 inch wide, in thin slices
250g/^{1}/2lb fresh mushrooms (sliced)
3 tablespoons of butter
1 tablespoon of oil
2 onions, finely chopped
1 glass of dry white wine
150ml/^{1}/4 pint beef stock
275ml/^{1}/2 pint double or whipping cream
Salt and freshly ground pepper

Heat 2 tablespoons of the butter in a heavy-bottomed casserole. Sauté the onions until translucent, then add the sliced mushrooms and cook for five minutes, until slightly brown. Remove and put to one side. In the same casserole add one tablespoon of butter and one of oil and gently sauté the beef fillet. Two to three minutes on each side should be sufficient, the inside of the meat should remain red.

Set the beef to one side. Discard the cooking fat. Then add the wine and stock to the casserole, scrape up the juices and cook over a high heat until the liquid is reduced. Stir in the cream. Return the mushrooms and onions to the casserole and then the beef. Heat gently for three minutes. Be careful not to overcook the meat, it should be pink and not well done.

Serve with rice and a green salad.

Poultry

Chicken is a very versatile meat – it can be steamed, grilled, fried, roasted, poached, and barbecued. But with storage onboard being a continual problem, whole chickens in the freezer or fridge take up considerable space. Therefore on longer trips it is wise to joint the chickens or duck before storing. Boneless, skinless chicken breasts are also great space savers on a boat. Try to buy organic chicken, which has much more flavour. Although poussins do not have an enormous amount of flavour, if stuffed with half a lemon and covered with dried mixed herbs, they are quite delicious.

Chicken with Mushrooms and Garlic

This is always popular, it can be made quickly and is delicious to eat.

Serves four

4 chicken breasts, cut into bite-size pieces
200g/7oz mushrooms, chopped
2 tablespoons butter
3 cloves of garlic, finely chopped
1 tablespoon parsley, chopped
275ml/^{1}/2 pint double cream
Salt and freshly ground pepper

Heat the butter in a frying pan, sauté the garlic and parsley. Then add the mushrooms and continue to cook gently for two minutes. Add the chicken and sauté for a further ten minutes, stirring all the time, until the chicken is cooked. Pour in the double cream and bring to the simmer. Season with salt and pepper.

Serve with farfalle and a green vegetable.

Fricassée de Poulet de Coco
(Chicken in Coconut Milk Sauce and Quince Jam)

This is a variation of a dish which is popular in Martinique, but the ingredients can be easily found elsewhere.

Serves four

1 medium-size free range chicken
1 lemon
2 tablespoons of butter
2 sprigs of thyme
1 red onion, chopped
1 clove of garlic, chopped
1 handful of raisins
440ml/14oz can of coconut milk (unsweetened)
1 tablespoon of mild curry powder (or stronger depending on taste)
1 tablespoon of ground coriander
1 tablespoon of quince jam
Salt and freshly ground pepper

Preheat oven to 200°C/400°F/Gas Mark 6

Cut the lemon in half and put inside the chicken with the thyme. Smear the bird with butter and season with salt and pepper. Place on a baking tray and put into the preheated oven. Cook for approximately one hour basting from time to time.

Meanwhile sauté the onions and garlic until translucent then add the curry powder and coriander. Cook for 3 minutes, stir in the quince jam then add the coconut milk. Simmer gently, finally adding the raisins. Put to one side until the chicken is ready, then gently bring back to the simmer.

When the chicken is cooked cut into pieces, place on a serving dish and pour over the coconut milk sauce.

Serve with rice.

Chicken Breasts with Mascarpone and Raisins

A very simple to make but tasty dish, ideal for the moments when it has been too rough to cook. It can be whipped up quickly in the calm of the port.

Serves four

4 chicken breasts with skin
4 tablespoons of mascarpone cheese
(If you cannot find mascarpone then it may be replaced with cream cheese mixed with one tablespoon of double cream to lighten the consistency)
1 tablespoon of olive oil
1 tablespoon of pine nuts
1 handful of raisins
1 clove of garlic finely chopped
Salt and freshly ground pepper

Preheat the oven to 230°C/450°F/Gas Mark 8

Mix the garlic, raisins, pine nuts and mascarpone cheese together and season with salt and pepper. Loosen the skin on the chicken and place a tablespoon of the mixture in the pocket under the skin of each breast. Heat the oil in a frying pan and brown the breasts on all sides. Put the chicken in an earthenware dish and place in the preheated oven. Bake for 20 minutes.

Serve with a green vegetable and boiled new potatoes.

Poulet à l'Estragon et Citron
(Chicken with Tarragon and Lemon)

This is the traditional recipe for Tarragon Chicken but with an extra zest of lemon.

Serves four

1 medium-size free range chicken
75g/3oz butter
1 tablespoon of lemon juice
1 lemon
1 bunch of fresh tarragon
275ml/$^1\!/2$ pint double cream
Salt and freshly ground pepper

Preheat oven to 200°C/400°F/Gas Mark 6

Mix the butter with salt and pepper and some lemon juice, then add the freshly chopped tarragon. Keep a few sprigs of chopped tarragon for later. Spread the mixture all over the chicken. Cut the lemon in quarters and place inside the bird.

Put the chicken in a roasting pan and place in the oven for 1-1$^1\!/2$ hours, basting it from time to time.

When the chicken is ready, remove from the roasting pan and keep warm. Meanwhile remove the fat from the tray, add the remaining chopped sprigs of tarragon and then cream, stirring all the time. Bring it to simmering point. Cut the chicken into pieces, place on a platter and pour over the sauce.

Serve with rice and a green salad.

Poussin au Citron

A very straightforward dish to make should you be lucky enough to find some poussin in the market.

Serves four

4 poussins (if small) or 2 large
2 lemons (unwaxed if possible)
2 teaspoons dried mixed herbs
2 tablespoons of butter
Salt and freshly ground pepper

Preheat oven to 200°C/400°F/Gas Mark 6

Mix the butter with the salt and pepper and the dried mixed herbs. Cover the poussins with the mixture. Cut the lemons into quarters and place inside each of the poussins. Roast in a preheated oven for approximately 45 minutes.

Serve with rice and a green vegetable.

Duck Breasts with Balsamic Vinegar and Cranberries

The combination of the balsamic vinegar and cranberries make an excellent sauce for this quick, easy to make recipe. However this is not a dish one can leave to simmer away, so make sure you can be in the galley for 30 minutes, without being called on deck. If you don't have any cranberry jam, substitute any jam or your choice.

Serves four

4 duck breasts
1 tablespoon of virgin olive oil
4 tablespoons of balsamic vinegar
110g/4oz fresh cranberries or cranberry jam
75g/3oz of brown sugar

Heat the oil in a frying pan, place the duck breasts in the oil, skin face down and cook for five minutes on a high heat until the skin is slightly brown. Reduce the heat and cook for a further ten minutes. After ten minutes drain the excess oil from the pan and turn the breasts over adding the balsamic vinegar and the fresh cranberries and brown sugar. (If you are using cranberry jam then it should be added 2 minutes before the end, and omitting the brown sugar). Cook for a further ten minutes.

Serve with the sauce and perhaps new potatoes and green beans.

Roast Duck with Orange Glaze

This is an easy recipe but make sure you have some good orange marmalade.

Serves four

1 duck weighing 2.25-3kg/5-6^1/2lbs
2 tablespoons of marmalade
2 tablespoons of port
1 orange

Preheat the oven to 220°C/425°F/Gas Mark 7

Prick the flesh of the duck with a fork. Place half the orange inside the cavity of the duck. Season with salt and pepper, place in a roasting tray then roast for 20 minutes. Reduce the temperature to 180°C/350°F/Gas Mark 4 and continue to roast for 2^1/2 hours. Check the fat in the tray from time to time and remove into a bowl.
   Make a glaze by melting the marmalade and port together. Ten minutes before the duck is ready brush the glaze over the skin and return to the oven.

Remove the duck from the oven.

Decorate with the remaining half orange and some watercress if available.

Facing page: Monkfish Kebabs with Mushrooms and Bacon (page 141).

BARBECUES

Over the years we saw various barbecues burning away on the sterns of other boats but we were always rather reticent to invest in one, thinking of the danger of hot coals burning teak decks, or shards being blown into the sails. However, with the invention of gas run barbecues these problems are a thing of the past. It is a marvellous way for cooking fresh fish or meat and we have found it to be a great alternative to cooking in the galley when temperatures soar.

Most of the recipes that follow are for a variety of grilled fish and meat with various marinades, or salsas. When planning a barbecue try to keep it simple and decide on one type of fish or meat, so the cooking time is the same for everything.

Marinating

When marinating always use a non-reactive container, i.e. glass or ceramic. Avoid plastic containers which will stain and pick up odours. Probably the best suggestion on board is to place the items in a large zip-lock plastic bag, or try using a bio bag, which can be thrown away after use.

Bacteria such as salmonella live between 45°F and 140°F, therefore marinate poultry in the fridge. Do not leave it out of the fridge for longer than 30 minutes.

One important point to remember is never re-use a marinade. When marinating meat some of the blood will mix into the marinade and there could be a risk of salmonella bacteria, so throw away after use.

If you are going to use your marinade to baste on the grill, then bring it to the boil to kill any bacteria present.

Marinated Tuna Steaks

Bluefin tuna, which is found in the Mediterranean, is ideal for this recipe. This was one of the recipes we used when we wanted a change from sashimi on our trip from Menorca to Gibraltar. The tuna should only be grilled for 2 minutes on each side.

Serves six

1 tuna, weighing about 1.5 k/4 ^{1}/2lbs. Cut the steaks so they weigh about 200g/7oz each and are 1.5cm/^{3}/4^{1}in thick
4 cloves of garlic, peeled and chopped
2 small dried red chillies, seeds removed
1 tablespoon of dried mixed herbs
200ml/7fl oz white wine
3 tablespoons of virgin olive oil
Juice of four lemons
Salt and freshly ground pepper

Rub the garlic, red chillies and dried mixed herbs into the fish and place the steaks in a large container. Mix the white wine, olive oil, lemon juice, salt and pepper together and pour over the steaks. Leave to marinate for at least one hour, turning the steaks from time to time.
Make sure that your barbecue is very hot and sear the steaks for two minutes on both sides.

Serve immediately, perhaps with a salsa sauce, see page 136.

Grilled Red Mullet with Salsa

The salsa recipe served with this red mullet can be used as an accompaniment to most grilled fish dishes. If you don't have any fresh peppers or chillies, then look into your store cupboard and use a can of chopped tomatoes and dried chillies.

Serves four

4 x 350g/12oz red mullet (approximate weight)

Salsa
2 tablespoons virgin olive oil
1 clove of garlic, peeled and chopped
2 red peppers, seeded and chopped
1 chilli pepper, seeded and chopped (or 2 small dried chillies,crumbled)
2 ripe tomatoes, peeled and chopped (or 1 can of chopped tomatoes)
2 tablespoons dried mixed herbs
Salt and pepper

For the Salsa
Heat the olive oil in a small saucepan, then add the garlic and cook until it starts to brown. Add the chilli and tomatoes and cook for 30 minutes. Then add the peppers and continue cooking for a further ten minutes.
Season with salt and pepper. Put to one side.

Prepare the mullet, snip off the fins, and remove the scales and gut the fish. Season, then place on the hot barbecue and grill the fish for 4- 5 minutes, until cooked.

Serve with the salsa.

Swordfish Kebabs

Tuna could also be used instead of swordfish.

Serves four

1.25–1.5kg/2^1/2–3lb swordfish steaks
1 red pepper, sliced into thick strips
1 green pepper, sliced into thick strips
2 red onions, cut into wedges

Marinade
Juice of one lemon
150ml/5fl oz virgin olive oil
2 cloves of garlic, peeled and crushed
1 tablespoon of chopped ginger
Salt and pepper

Mix the ingredients for the marinade together. Cut the steaks into bite-size cubes. Pour over the marinade and leave for one hour in the fridge.
Remove the fish from the marinade and then alternate the pepper, fish and onion on the skewers. Lay the kebabs on the grill and cook for 6–8 minutes. Turn the kebabs half way through cooking, basting from time to time with a little of the marinade.

Grilled Squid

The body of these squid are stuffed with their tentacles, plus a little garlic and parsley. It's a dish we discovered in Portugal on our way down from the River Hamble to Menorca. A very simple recipe, but try to buy small squid.

Serves four

700g/1 1/2lb of small squid
1 handful of parsley, finely chopped
30g/1oz of butter
2 cloves of garlic, finely chopped
2 tablespoons olive oil
4 toothpicks
Juice of one lemon
Salt and pepper

Clean the squid, following the instructions on page 96. Cut off the tentacles and chop them into small pieces. Mix them with the butter, parsley, garlic, salt and pepper. Stuff the squid with the mixture and close the end with a wooden toothpick.

Brush the squid and the grill with olive oil. Make sure your barbecue is really hot, then grill the squid for a total of about 15 minutes.

Serve with lemon juice.

Barbecued Drumsticks

The important part of this recipe is the marinade. The quantity is suitable for twelve drumsticks. For the best results leave the chicken to marinate overnight. However, it is quite important to pre-cook drumsticks in the oven for about 15 minutes. This cuts down barbecuing time and ensures the chicken is thoroughly cooked through.

Serves four

12 chicken drumsticks
150ml/5fl oz of soy sauce
3 tablespoons of olive oil
1 tablespoon Dijon mustard
1 tablespoon clear honey
4 cloves of garlic, peeled and crushed
1 tablespoon dried mixed herbs

Put the mustard into a bowl, and slowly add the olive oil, stirring until it amalgamates. Then add the soy sauce, honey, garlic and dried mixed herbs. Pierce the drumsticks several times with a fork and arrange them in a shallow dish. Pour over the marinade, making sure the drumsticks are well coated. If possible leave to marinate for 12 hours turning from time to time.

Preheat the oven to 180°C/350°F/Gas Mark 4

Cook the drumsticks in the oven for 15 minutes and then cook on a barbecue for about 10 minutes on each side.

Serve with potato salad and a green salad.

Barbecued Spare Ribs

Pre-cook the ribs in the oven, before finalising the cooking on the barbecue. If possible marinate the ribs overnight. If you are on a longer trip, and are not able to barbecue then they can be cooked entirely in your oven.

Serves four

1.25kg/2^1/2lb of pork spare ribs

Marinade
4 tablespoons soy sauce
4 tablespoons clear honey
3 cloves of garlic, peeled and crushed
2 tablespoons ketchup
1 tablespoons dried mixed herbs
Juice of one lemon
Salt and pepper

Mix all the ingredients of the marinade together.
    Put the spare ribs in a large shallow dish and pour over the marinade. Leave overnight.

Preheat the oven to 180°C/350°F/Gas Mark 4

Put the ribs together with the marinade in a roasting tin, cover with tin foil and bake for one hour. Uncover and cook for 20 minutes, then remove the ribs from the oven and grill on the barbecue for a total of 15 minutes, until they are cooked.

Monkfish Kebabs with Mushrooms and Bacon

The combination of bacon, mushrooms and monkfish makes a delicious and succulent dish.

Serves four

750g/1¹/2lb of monkfish fillet cut into cubes
1 red pepper, sliced and cut into squares
1 red onion, cut in quarters
200g/7oz mushrooms
110g/4oz bacon, sliced and cut into squares
Salt and freshly ground pepper

Wooden skewers soaked in water for 30 minutes, so they won't burn on the grill.

Starting with the red pepper, thread the red onion, monkfish, mushroom and bacon alternatively on each skewer and brush with olive oil. Place on a very hot grill and cook for about five minutes.

Pork Kebabs with Apple and Onion

This is not quite a food locker recipe but most sailors usually have apples and onions aboard, and I nearly always have pork tenderloin in the freezer.

Serves four

1kg/2lb of pork tenderloin, cut into squares
2 apples, cut into quarters and then squares
 (the sharp Granny Smith variety work well)
2 large red onions, cut in quarters

Wooden skewers soaked in water for 30 minutes, so they won't burn on the grill.

Starting with the onion, thread the pork tenderloin and apple alternatively through the skewers. Place on a medium hot grill for 30 to 40 minutes turning from time to time.

Serve with potatoes in their jackets and green salad.

Monkfish and Scallop Kebab

Monkfish, which is sometimes known as the 'poor man's lobster', is boneless and therefore perfect for making kebabs and for barbecuing. If you do not have a barbecue then use a griddle pan.

Serves four

8 medium scallops
350g/12oz monkfish tail
140g/5oz softened butter
Lemon juice

Wooden skewers (soak the skewers in water before using, so they don't burn).

Cut the monkfish into scallop-sized cubes. Start by threading a scallop, followed by the monkfish onto the skewers. Allow two scallops per person. Season with salt and pepper and brush the kebabs thickly with softened butter.

Heat the barbecue or griddle pan until very hot before placing the kebabs on the grill. Cook for 3 minutes on either side.

Facing page: Gratin Dauphinois (page 151).

VEGETABLES

Roasting is not only a wonderfully effortless way of cooking a large variety of vegetables but is also terrific at sealing in the natural flavours. You can roast four or five vegetables in one tray and the results are always succulent and tasty.

Vegetable buying is something that has to be planned carefully before you depart. Having first chosen your menus, then select the vegetables and store them carefully. Most vegetables store well, although vacuum packing will increase their shelf life. Alternatively, buy the Green Bags (also known as bio bags) mentioned in the Storage chapter, they double the life of fruit, vegetables, meat and fish.

Herbs

One of the problems on a longer trip is being able to keep fresh herbs. The only potted herb I keep on board is basil. However, all herbs freeze well and this is particularly useful for the herbs that lose their flavour when dried, such as basil, chives, dill leaves and parsley. Wash and dry the herbs and pack into small labelled polythene bags, or use bio bags. Put the bags into a container to prevent the herbs from being damaged in the freezer. If you do not have a freezer, then pack into bags and remove as much air as possible before storing in the fridge. They should last for up to two weeks, or longer in bio bags.

One of the joys of cooking on board is that you can experiment with a variety of herbs in different dishes especially when you have just run out of the herb you were intending to use. The local corner shop is not just around the corner, so you have to use your store locker for inspiration.

Bear in mind that one tablespoon of fresh herbs is more or less the equivalent of $1/2$ tablespoon of dried herbs.

Roasted Vegetables

This recipe can be varied depending on what you have found in the market.

Serves six

500g/1lb courgettes (zucchini)
12 shallots, peeled
3 red peppers
500g/1lb potatoes, peeled and cut in quarters
3 aubergines (eggplant)
3 tablespoons of virgin olive oil

Preheat the oven to 220°C/425°F/Gas Mark 7

Cut the vegetables into large pieces and spread them out in a single layer in a large earthenware baking dish. Sprinkle with salt and toss them in the olive oil. Bake for about fifty minutes, turning occasionally. The vegetables are ready when they are tender and brown and the potatoes are cooked through.

Broccoli with Anchovies

Serves four

1kg/2.2lb of broccoli cut into florets
50g/2oz butter
3 cloves of garlic, peeled and sliced
6 anchovy fillets chopped
50g/2oz of Parmesan cheese, grated
Juice of one lemon
Salt and pepper

Blanch the broccoli in boiling water for about two minutes. Drain and transfer to a serving bowl. Meanwhile, melt the butter in a saucepan and gently fry the garlic until it begins to colour. Add the anchovies and the lemon juice. Heat until the butter foams. Pour the mixture over the broccoli and sprinkle with grated Parmesan cheese.

Courgettes (Zucchini) with Red Onions

Courgettes, or zucchini, are another good vegetable to have onboard as their shelf life is two to three weeks. This is a quick dish to prepare, ideal to serve with grilled or barbecued meat.

Serves four

750g/1¹/2lb courgettes, diced
2 tablespoons virgin olive oil
1 large red onion, peeled and chopped
2 teaspoons dried mixed herbs

Heat the oil in a frying pan and sauté the onions. When they are translucent add the courgettes and the dried mixed herbs and cook for about five minutes, stirring from time to time until they are cooked, but still firm. Serve immediately.

Catalan Spinach

This dish makes a great starter. As a lunch meal you could serve it with eggs, either poached or hardboiled. Frozen spinach works equally well with this recipe.

Serves four

500g/1lb fresh or frozen spinach
4 tablespoons olive oil
2 tablespoons pine nuts
2 tablespoons raisins soaked in 1 tablespoon of sherry
2 cloves of garlic, peeled and chopped
2 tablespoons of double cream (optional)

Put the fresh spinach into a covered pan with very little water and a small amount of salt and cook for five minutes. If you are using frozen spinach then cook according to the directions. While the spinach is cooking, strain the raisins and fry them in the olive oil with the chopped garlic and pine nuts until the nuts are golden. Drain the spinach well and add to the frying pan with the raisins, nuts and garlic. Season to taste.

Optional: At this point you may add two tablespoons of double or whipping cream.

Gratin Dauphinois

This is one of the traditional gratin dishes, always very popular, and a great accompaniment to roast leg of lamb.

Serves four

Pre-heat oven to 200°C/400°F/Gas Mark/6

500g/1lb potatoes, peeled
250ml/1/2 pint double or whipping cream
400ml/14fl oz of milk
1 clove of garlic, peeled and sliced
100g/3 1/2 oz Gruyère, or any other hard cheese

Parboil the potatoes for ten minutes, then cool and slice thinly. Put the milk and cream into a large saucepan and bring to the boil. Add the garlic slivers and seasoning then simmer for a couple of minutes. Put the sliced potatoes into a shallow earthenware dish, sprinkling the cheese between the layers. Keep some cheese for the top layer. Pour the milk and cream over the potatoes and sprinkle over the remaining cheese.

Bake for 20 minutes or until golden brown.

Oven Roasted Potatoes with Garlic and Rosemary

These potatoes are delicious. Just pop them into the oven whilst the barbecue is heating and serve them crisp and brown.

Serves four

750g/1¹/₂lb medium size new potatoes (unpeeled)
2 tablespoons olive oil
4 cloves of garlic, peeled and chopped
2 tablespoons chopped rosemary
Salt and pepper

Pre-heat the oven to 230°C/450°F/Gas Mark 8

Put 2 tablespoons of olive oil into a roasting tin, and pop into the oven to heat through.

Cut the potatoes into cubes about ¹/₂inch/1cm. Remove the tin from the oven, then carefully add the potatoes into the hot oil. Sprinkle in the rosemary and chopped garlic and mix well making sure the potatoes are well covered with the oil.

Place the tin at the top of the oven and roast for 25–30 minutes or until the potatoes are golden brown. Season with salt and pepper.

Glazed carrots

Carrots are one of the most useful vegetables on board. Not only can they be served as an accompanying vegetable, they can also can be used as a base for stews and roasts, or even eaten raw. Their longevity is also a plus, as most carrots will last for up to three to four weeks in a cool dry environment.

Serves four

450g/1lb carrots, sliced into large julienne (or straw-like strips)
50g/2oz butter
1 teaspoon caraway seeds, finely ground
Juice of one lemon
2 tablespoons brown sugar

Bring a pan of salted water to the boil and add the carrots. Cook for three minutes before straining. Meanwhile melt the butter and add the brown sugar, carrots, caraway seed and lemon juice and cook for a few minutes. Serve immediately.

La Ratatouille Niçoise

This is a very useful recipe and one of my favourite vegetable dishes. It's a marvellous accompaniment to both fish and meat dishes and if you make enough you can serve it cold the following day as a salad. The correct way to cook ratatouille is to cook the vegetables in separate saucepans, as their timing is different, but this is not practical in a galley. The way around this is to add the vegetables according to their cooking time, but make sure your saucepan is large enough.

Serves four

6 tablespoons olive oil
2 large onions, diced
4 cloves of garlic, peeled and chopped
1 green pepper, diced
1 red pepper, diced
2 medium sized aubergines, diced
2 courgettes, diced
4 ripe tomatoes, peeled seeded and chopped
   (or a 400g tin of chopped tomatoes)
2 teaspoons thyme
1 handful of basil, chopped
1 tablespoon parsley, chopped

Heat the oil in a heavy bottomed saucepan, add the onions and garlic and sauté until the onions are transparent. Then add the diced peppers and aubergines and cook for five minutes before adding the courgettes and tomatoes. Simmer the vegetables for about thirty minutes. Finally add the thyme, basil and parsley. Cook uncovered for about 20–30 minutes, until most of the juice has evaporated.

Serve hot or cold.

Aubergines (Eggplant) with Onions and Garlic

Aubergines last a relatively long time. Up to two weeks normally and up to three weeks in a bio bag. This is a great dish to serve with roast lamb.

Serves four

500g/1lb aubergines (eggplant) cubed
5 tablespoons of virgin olive oil
3 shallots, finely chopped
1 handful of parsley, finely chopped
1 handful of pine nuts
3 cloves of garlic, peeled and chopped

Put the cubed aubergines in a colander and sprinkle with salt. Allow to stand for an hour, then rinse well and pat dry. Heat the olive oil in a heavy based saucepan, then add the aubergines, stirring from time to time, adding extra olive oil if needed. When the aubergines are slightly brown add the pine nuts, parsley, garlic and shallots and cook for a few minutes until the shallots are translucent and the garlic slightly brown.

Season with salt and pepper.

DESSERTS
AND BREAD

Like all dishes prepared aboard a boat, desserts have to be kept simple. By using store locker ingredients you can easily conjure up a delightful surprise at the end of a day. Some of the recipes are cold so they may be made earlier in the day and popped into the fridge.

A nutty fruit cake has been included but remember to take all the ingredients. If you are embarking on a long trip you will have plenty of time to bake – and there is nothing quite like a slice of moist fruit cake to relieve the pangs of hunger that may strike at four in the morning.

Crêpes/pancakes are also fun to make as well as being delicious to eat. As we crossed the Atlantic, our son became a whizz at tossing them, even in fairly rough conditions. Make sure that you have several cans of condensed milk and ample supplies of caster sugar before you take off on a trip of any duration.

As apples store well, I have included several recipes using this fruit.

Jean's Brownies

I have had to include a brownie recipe. Not only are you likely to have the ingredients in your store cupboard, but brownies are always extremely popular with everyone. Not surprisingly, they always seem to disappear far too quickly.

60g/2oz of unsweetened chocolate
125g/4¹/2oz of butter
200g/7oz of sugar
2 eggs
75g/3oz of flour
A few drops of vanilla essence
75g/3oz of chopped walnuts (optional)

Preheat the oven to 190°C/375°F/Gas Mark 5

Butter a 20 x 24cm (8in x 9¹/2in) rectangular baking tin. Melt the butter and chocolate in a double boiler. Take off the stove and add the sugar and eggs beating at the same time. Then add the flour, vanilla essence and walnuts. Mix well. Bake in the oven for 20–25 minutes.

Ricotta and Mascarpone Cream

A wonderfully simple dessert. It's a dream to make and a dream to eat.

Serves four

250g/8oz ricotta cheese
50g/2oz mascarpone cheese
3 teaspoons of strong, brewed coffee
75g/3oz caster sugar
3 tablespoons of dark rum

Put the ricotta cheese and mascarpone in a blender with the sugar and coffee and blend until smooth. Add the rum then pour the mixture into separate dessert dishes and chill for two hours before serving.

(If you do not have a blender this may be mixed with a hand beater.)

Quince or Guava with Cream Cheese

This is definitely a store locker recipe. You can use either quince or guava depending on where you happen to find yourself. Quince paste, which comes from Spain and is known as Membrillo, can be found in good delicatessen shops. Guava paste may be found in many of the Caribbean supermarkets. I've found this to be the ideal dessert for those moments when you hadn't planned to serve a dessert but a member of the crew has a very sweet tooth.....

1 tin of quince or guava paste
350g/12oz of cream cheese or ricotta cheese

Cut a few slices of quince or guava and arrange on plate with slices of ricotta or cream cheese, and serve.

Crêpes

This is a basic crêpe mixture to which you can add your favourite topping. Make sure you have the right size frying pan, it should not be more than 18cms (7in) in diameter. This recipe should make about 20 crêpes.

225g/8oz of flour
1 tablespoon of sugar
3 eggs
425ml/¾ pint of milk
2 tablespoons of melted butter
2 tablespoons of cognac
Salt

Beat the eggs. Sift the flour and then add the sugar and salt. Add the eggs to the flour mixture. Slowly mix in the melted butter, milk and cognac. If you find the mixture is lumpy, then strain it through a sieve. Leave the mixture to stand for two hours. When ready to cook the batter should be thin, if it is too thick then add some water. Grease the frying pan with butter. Using a tablespoon, pour the mixture into the pan. You will need about 2 tablespoons for each crêpe. Cook over a medium heat for about one minute on each side.

Make sure that you re-grease the pan with butter and reheat it between cooking each pancake.

Ideas for fillings/toppings:
Lemon pancakes – lemon juice with caster sugar
Maple syrup
Strawberry jam
Nutella

Baked Apples with Raisins

Another simple dish and ideal for a long crossing as apples can be stored so easily. If you are unable to buy cooking apples, try and find the tartest apple available.

Serves four

4 medium size cooking apples, cored
110g/4oz of brown sugar
A handful of raisins

Preheat the oven to 180°C/350°F/Gas Mark 4

Remove the core of each apple. With a sharp knife, cut a ring around the middle of each apple, making sure you go through the skin. This stops them bursting all over the oven as they heat up.

Put a mixture of raisins and brown sugar in the centre of each apple then sprinkle with the remaining sugar. Place the apples in an ovenproof dish. Pour some water over the apples, to a depth of about half an inch.

Bake in the oven for about 45 minutes until the apples are soft. Serve immediately with crème fraîche or ice cream.

Apple and Blackberry Crumble

This is a quick, easy recipe, which can literally be thrown together for a cold hungry crew at the end of a hard day's sailing.

Serves four

450g/1lb of cooking apples, peeled and sliced
225g/1/2lb of blackberries
3 tablespoons of brown sugar
Juice of one orange

For the crumble topping
170g/6oz of plain flour
110g/4oz of butter
55g/2oz of granulated sugar
Pinch of salt
1 teaspoon of ground cinnamon

Preheat the oven to 200°C/400°F/Gas Mark 6

Mix the apples, blackberries, brown sugar and orange juice together in an ovenproof dish. Sift the flour and ground cinnamon into a bowl, then add the sugar and salt. Rub in the butter until the mixture resembles coarse breadcrumbs. Sprinkle the flour mixture over the top of the fruit.

Bake in the oven for 45 minutes or until the top is slightly brown.

Old Fashioned American Fruit Pie

A very easy pie to make and ideal for galley cooking as no baking tins are required and no tops have to be cut. For the fruit filling you can use anything you have to hand, but here I have made it with apples.

Quick pie crust pasty
110g/4oz unsalted butter (room temperature)
150g/5oz plain flour, sifted
10g/$^{1}/_{2}$oz caster sugar
Pinch of salt
5fl oz/140ml cold water
1 egg yolk, beaten
2 tablespoons of semolina

For the filling
700g1$^{1}/_{2}$lbs of tart apples
75g/3oz caster sugar
1 teaspoon of cinnamon
1 egg white
Demerera sugar

Sift the flour into a large bowl, then add the other dry ingredients. Combine the butter with the flour until it resembles bread crumbs.

Gradually add the cold water until the dough pulls away from the bowl. Place the pastry in a polythene bag in the fridge for 20 minutes.

Then preheat the oven to 190°C/375°F/Gas Mark 5.

Remove the dough from the fridge and roll out to a 12in circle (or as round as you can make it). Transfer the pastry to the centre of a greased baking tray. Paint the base of the pie with the egg yolk, then sprinkle over the semolina. This will prevent the crust from getting soggy from the fruit filling.

Fill the pie with the filling of your choice, in this case apple slices. Place the fruit in the centre of the pastry. Sprinkle with sugar, and cinnamon, dot with butter, then fold the pastry up over the apples.

continued over

Brush the pastry with the egg white and sprinkle with some demerara sugar. Bake in the oven for 45 minutes until the crust is golden.

Serve with crème fraîche or ice cream.

Ideas for alternative fillings

Apricots and almonds
700g/1 1/2lbs fresh stoned apricots, cut in half, with some slivered almonds

Fresh raspberries and redcurrants
675g/1 1/4lb raspberries and 110g/4oz redcurrants with 50g/2oz sugar

Apple and blackberry
450g/1lb tart apples and 225g/8oz blackberries with 50g/2oz sugar

The *Jupiter Moon* Nutty Fruit Cake

This really is a marvellous nutty fruit cake which, once made, will store indefinitely – that is if anyone will allow it to. It's ideal food for boosting the energy levels. If you don't have or can't find some of the dried ingredients at your supermarket, then substitute with an alternative.

125g/4oz whole cashew nuts, shelled
125g/4oz whole Brazil nuts, shelled
125g/4oz shelled walnuts, halved
125g/4oz mixture of glacé fruit, i.e. peaches, pears, pineapple or whatever you can find. If unavailable then replace with chopped mixed peel
50g/2oz chopped dried dates or figs
50g/2oz chopped mixed peel
110g/4oz raisins
50g/2oz glace cherries
75g/3oz of caster sugar
50g/2oz flour
1/4 teaspoon of baking powder
1/2 teaspoon of vanilla essence
3 tablespoons of brandy
2 eggs, beaten
Pinch of salt

Preheat the oven to 140°C/275°F Mark 1.

Sift the flour, sugar, baking powder and salt into a large bowl, then add the fruit and nuts, mixing well to make sure they are all covered with the flour. Beat the eggs then add the brandy and vanilla essence. Pour this mixture into the dried ingredients. Mix well, it will be quite stiff.

Grease a 22cm x 8cm (8½in x 3 in) bread tin, or a round 18 cm (7in) tin, and pour in the mixture. Bake in the oven for 2½ hours.
   Remove from the oven, allow to cool for ten minutes before removing from the tin and placing on a cake rack to cool.

Easy Wholemeal Bread

This recipe is an adaptation of Doris Grant's famous loaf. It is simple to make as it does not require kneading and only has to rise once, making it especially suitable for baking in the galley. Another advantage to this loaf is that it is delicious with soups or for making sandwiches.

700g/1½lbs stoneground wholemeal flour
2 level teaspoons sea salt
2 teaspoons of honey
7gm/¼oz sachet of dried yeast
570ml/1 pint tepid water
1 tablespoon of sesame seeds

Grease a 900g/2lb loaf tin
Preheat the oven to 200°C/400°F/Gas Mark6.

Gently warm the flour in the oven to room temperature, then put it in a large ovenproof bowl. Meanwhile mix the honey and yeast with 100ml of the tepid water. Make a well in the flour. Pour the yeast mixture and the remaining water into the well in the flour. Mix with your hands and continue until you have a smooth dough that should leave the sides of the bowl.

Put the dough into the prepared tin and cover with a damp tea towel. Leave it to rise in a warm place for 40-50 minutes. By this time the dough should nearly reach the top of the tin.

Sprinkle the dough with the sesame seeds and bake in the preheated oven for 45 minutes. Remove the bread from the tin and tap it. It should sound hollow. If it sounds heavy return it to the oven for a further five minutes then test again. When the bread sounds hollow, place it upside down in the oven (without the tin). Bake for a further 5-10 minutes.

Cool the bread on a wire rack completely before cutting.

This bread can be kept for up to one month in the freezer.

Facing page: Pesto Sauce (page 177).

SAUCES
AND BUTTERS

Just as soups and stocks have their place in the galley, so too do sauces and butters. They are quick to make and do much to enhance the taste of steak or fresh fish. The following are the most popular sauces and butters, most of which can be altered to give a different flavour by adding ingredients to the basic recipe.

Béchamel Sauce

This is probably the most important and useful of all sauces, being the basis for a whole range of other sauces. It is extremely simple, and all the ingredients should be in your store locker.

2 tablespoons butter
2 tablespoons plain flour
570ml/1 pint milk
Salt and pepper

Melt the butter in a thick bottom saucepan. Remove from the heat and stir in the flour, return to the heat and cook gently for three to five minutes stirring constantly until the flour is cooked. Remove from the heat and add a little milk stirring vigorously. Keep adding the milk, stirring constantly until you have a good smooth sauce. Return the pan to the heat and let the sauce cook, stirring from time to time, making sure that it does not stick to the bottom of the pan. The sauce is ready when you can see a glaze on the spoon.
Season with salt and freshly ground black pepper.

Using the Béchamel Sauce as a base, you can make a variety of sauces, such as Sauce Mornay, Sauce Aurore, and Sauce à la Crème.

Sauce Mornay (Cheese Sauce)

Suitable for egg, fish, poultry and pasta and macaroni mixtures.

570ml/1pint Béchamel Sauce
2-4 tablespoons of grated Swiss cheese (or Parmesan)
Salt and pepper
Pinch of nutmeg

Bring the Béchamel sauce to the boil. Remove from the heat and beat in the cheese until it has melted and blended with the sauce. Season to taste with salt, pepper and nutmeg.

Sauce Aurore

An excellent sauce for fish, shellfish, chicken and eggs.

570ml/1pint Béchamel Sauce
3 tablespoons of tomato purée
1 tablespoon of softened butter

Bring the Béchamel sauce to a simmer, slowly stir in the tomato purée to taste. Take off the heat and then stir in the butter just before serving.

Sauce à la Crème

A great rich sauce for fish, chicken dishes, and eggs.

570ml/1pt Béchamel Sauce
4 tablespoons double or whipping cream
A few drops of lemon juice
Salt and pepper

Bring the Béchamel sauce to the boil. Add the cream, being careful not to let the sauce boil. Then add a few drops of lemon juice.

Mayonnaise

Mayonnaise is another sauce to which various ingredients may be added to make alternative sauces such as Remoulade, Aioli, Sauce Tartar and Rouille.

For approximately 250ml/½ pint of mayonnaise, you will need the following:

Two egg yolks
250ml/½ pint virgin olive oil
Lemon juice or tarragon vinegar
1 teaspoon of Dijon mustard
Salt and pepper

Before starting the mayonnaise make sure all your ingredients are at room temperature, to keep the sauce from curdling.

Place the egg yolks in a bowl, with a little lemon juice or tarragon vinegar and blend well together. Add the oil drop by drop, stirring all the time. When you have added half the olive oil, add a little more lemon juice and the Dijon mustard.

By now the sauce should be a good consistency, so continue adding the olive oil in a slow steady flow, stirring all the time. Add more lemon juice or vinegar if necessary to taste, and season with salt and pepper.

If for some reason the sauce should curdle, break an egg, using only the yolk, into another bowl. Whisk the yolk and slowly add the curdled mayonnaise, little by little, stirring all the time. It should now take.

The mayonnaise will keep for the next day, if you whisk in a tablespoon of boiling water.

Sauce Rémoulade

This is a delicious sauce, especially served with fish, shellfish and lobster.

250ml/1/2 pint mayonnaise
2 tablespoons of finely chopped fresh tarragon or basil
1 tablespoon of finely chopped parsley
1 clove of garlic, peeled and finely chopped
1 tablespoon of Dijon mustard
2 small gherkins, finely chopped
Salt and freshly ground pepper

Combine all ingredients, chill and serve.

Aioli

Aioli, which is an excellent sauce to accompany shellfish, was traditionally made with olive oil and crushed garlic. However, in the following recipe mayonnaise is used.

250ml/1/2 pint mayonnaise
Six fat cloves of garlic, peeled

Crush the garlic to a smooth paste, then add the mayonnaise.

Sauce Tartare

This is a great sauce for grilled or fried fish.

250ml/1/2 pint mayonnaise
2 finely chopped gherkins
2 teaspoons of chopped capers
2 teaspoons of chopped parsley or tarragon
1 shallot, finely chopped

Combine all the above ingredients together and serve.

Sauce Rouille

In the South of France this is usually served with fish soup (such as Bouillabaisse) but it is also an excellent dip for prawns.

2 tablespoons of mayonnaise
2 tablespoons of olive oil
2 cloves of garlic peeled and crushed
2 teaspoons of tomato purée
2 teaspoons of hot paprika
1 pinch of cayenne pepper
Salt

Blend the paprika and the crushed garlic together, then slowly add the mayonnaise, tomato purée and olive oil. Season with salt. Sprinkle with the cayenne pepper and serve.

Simple Tomato Sauce

This is a great standby – in 20 minutes you have an easy and delicious sauce for pasta.

2 x 400g/14oz cans of tomatoes, chopped
3 tablespoons of virgin olive oil
3 cloves of garlic, peeled and chopped
A handful of fresh basil, or a tablespoon of dried mixed herbs
1 pinch of sugar
Salt and pepper

In a heavy bottomed saucepan, heat the oil and sauté the garlic, then add the canned tomatoes, basil or dried herbs, sugar, salt and pepper. Simmer uncovered for 20 minutes.

This will keep in the fridge for about four days and also freezes very well.

Salsa

See recipe on page 136.

Vinaigrette Sauce

1 tablespoon of vinegar (depending on the flavour your require this
could be tarragon or balsamic). Alternatively, you could use
lemon juice
1/2 clove of finely chopped garlic
1/4 teaspoon of honey (not necessary if you are using balsamic
vinegar)
3 tablespoons of virgin olive oil
Salt and pepper

Combine the vinegar with the chopped garlic and honey. Add the olive oil and season with salt and pepper.

Pesto Sauce

This is a very versatile sauce, which can be used with spaghetti or with meat. Traditionally pesto sauce was made with a mortar and pestle, but a blender does the job equally well.

1 large bunch of fresh basil, chopped
2 large cloves of garlic, crushed
50g/1¾oz of pine nuts
50g/1¾oz of grated Parmesan cheese
2 tablespoons of olive oil

Mix the basil leaves in a blender, or pound the leaves in a pestle and mortar. Add the pine nuts, crushed garlic and the cheese and when all the ingredients have formed a thick paste, add the olive oil, a little at a time, making sure you blend it well with the other ingredients.

If you wish to store the sauce, place it in a jar making sure it is covered with a layer of olive oil to preserve it. This should last up to three weeks in the fridge.

Butters

Butters are an easy way to enhance grilled meats or vegetables. They can be made in advance and stored in the fridge or freezer and brought out when required.

Garlic Butter

125g/4oz softened butter
2 cloves of garlic, peeled and crushed
1 tablespoon of parsley finely chopped
2 tablespoons of lemon juice
Salt and pepper

Mix the butter with the crushed garlic and finely chopped parsley, season to taste with lemon juice, salt and freshly ground black pepper. Chill.

Herb Butter

125g/4¹/₂oz softened butter
2 tablespoons of any mixture of fresh herbs, finely chopped
** (If using dried herbs, a teaspoon will be sufficient)**

Mix the butter with the herbs, season with salt and pepper. Chill.

SPECIAL
OCCASIONS

I thought it would be a good idea to include something on special occasions. When we were preparing for our trip across the Atlantic from Las Palmas in the Canary Islands, I realised that shortly after our departure it would be Thanksgiving. As both my partner and my son are American it seemed it would be in order to celebrate this occasion. Luckily Las Palmas is a marvellous place to prepare for an Atlantic trip, and equally wonderful is the fact they have a Corte Inglés supermarket. Someone did make the comparison that Corte Inglés's food hall could be called the Harrods Food Hall of Spain. A frozen turkey was found and popped into the freezer until the great day.

You may also find yourself in the middle of an ocean over Christmas so I have included a few recipes and tips for these festivities. However, before you leave make sure that you have shopped for all the necessary ingredients. You may not feel like making stuffing on board but fortunately there are some very good organic stuffing mixes on the market. The size of your turkey will not only depend on the size of your crew but also your oven. A 5kg to 6kg turkey should be sufficient for a crew of six. Not only should you check on the size of your oven and whether the turkey will fit, but also the size of the baking pan!

When you buy your turkey, if you are going to freeze it, then remove the giblets and freeze separately. Don't forget to put cranberry sauce on your shopping list, unfortunately fresh cranberries would not keep long enough.

Home made Christmas puddings are special but they do involve a lot of work and cooking time. These days there are some excellent ready-made Christmas puddings in the shops but I've included a recipe for brandy butter. It's simple to make but being home made it adds that extra something to a Christmas dessert.

Roast Turkey

This roast turkey is made with traditional pork stuffing, served with mashed potatoes instead of roast to save space in the oven, and green beans and glazed carrots.

4.5kg/10lb turkey
225g/8oz bacon
175g/6oz butter

For the stuffing
500g/1lb pork sausage meat, skinned
2 tablespoons white breadcrumbs
1 onion, finely chopped
1 tablespoon of dried sage
125g/4oz dried prunes, chopped and soaked in port or brandy
2 tablespoons chopped celery
50g/2oz chopped walnuts

Preheat the oven to 220°C/425°F/Gas Mark 7

Combine all the stuffing ingredients, then place inside the neck-end of the turkey. Make sure that your turkey is well defrosted and that both the stuffing and the bird are at room temperature. Arrange two sheets of foil on your roasting tin, one widthways and the other lengthways. Place the turkey on the foil. Rub the turkey with butter and season with salt and pepper. Lay the bacon over the breast and wrap the turkey in the foil.

Place the turkey in the preheated oven at a high temperature for 30 minutes, then lower the temperature to 170°C/325°F/Gas Mark 3 for 2½-3 hours, then remove the foil and cook uncovered for 30 minutes at 200°C/400°F/ Gas Mark 6.

Brandy Butter

You can replace the brandy with rum for this recipe.

175g/6oz unsalted butter (room temperature)
175g/6oz dark soft brown sugar
6 tablespoons of brandy or rum

Blend the butter and sugar until it becomes soft and creamy, then add the rum or brandy little by little, beating well. Cover and place in the fridge until required. It will keep for 2-3 weeks.

Whole Turbot or Brill baked in Sea Salt

This is an easy recipe, and quite impressive when served, but remember to buy a large amount of sea salt for your store locker.

Serves four to six

1 turbot or brill with head and tail, only the gut removed – 3kg/7lb
3kg/6lb of sea salt
Fresh rosemary (if not available, dried is fine)
3 cloves of garlic, peeled and chopped
Virgin olive oil
Lemon juice

Preheat oven to 220°C/425°F/Gas Mark 7

Cover the bottom of a baking tray with a layer of salt, and place the turbot or brill on the salt. Put the mixture of rosemary and garlic into the cavity of the fish and cover with the remaining salt. This should be about 1cm thick. Sprinkle lightly with a little water. Place in the preheated oven and bake for 25–35 minutes. Test to see if it is ready by inserting a skewer into the centre of the fish. If the skewer is warm the fish is cooked.

Allow to cool for five minutes then remove as much salt as possible.

Serve with olive oil and lemon juice and small new potatoes, if available.

Duck Legs Braised in Coconut Milk and Soy Sauce

This is a delicious dish, an adaptation from Peter Gordon's recipe in the Sugar Club cookbook. It's a special recipe for a special occasion but it can happily simmer away and doesn't require too much attention.

Serves four

Four duck legs
450ml/3⁄4 pint can of unsweetened coconut milk
75ml/3fl oz of soy sauce
4 red onions, peeled and sliced
6 cloves of garlic
1 cup of ginger, peeled and grated
1 stick of lemon grass (if available)

Preheat oven to 190°C/375°F/Gas Mark 5

Mix all the ingredients together except the duck legs, coconut milk and soy sauce. Place in an eathernware dish or casserole with a lid. Place the legs on top of the ingredients and then add the coconut milk and soy sauce. Cover with foil and then the lid and place in the oven. Check the legs after 1 1⁄2 hours, they should be tender. Remove the lid and the foil and return the dish to the oven for approximately 30 minutes. The duck legs are ready when the skin is brown.

Serve with rice.

Hardy's Pie

This is a really delicious dessert. Check your oven temperature before starting this recipe to make sure it stays at a low temperature. This is a dessert for very special occasions, and shouldn't be attempted in rough conditions!

For the meringue shell
3 egg whites
1/8th teaspoon of cream of tartar
Pinch of salt
175g/6oz granulated sugar
A few drops of vanilla essence
125g/4¹/₂oz finely chopped pecan nuts (or walnuts)

110g/4oz good cooking chocolate
3 tablespoons of strong, brewed coffee
A few drops of vanilla essence
158ml/6fl oz double cream

Preheat the oven to 150°C/300°F/Gas Mark 2

Beat the egg whites until foaming. Add the cream of tartar and a pinch of salt. Beat until the mixture makes soft peaks. Gradually add the sugar and beat until stiff. Add 1 teaspoon of vanilla. Fold in the chopped pecan nuts. Pour into a well-buttered 23cm (9in) pie dish and bake for 50–55 minutes. Leave to cool.

Meanwhile, melt the chocolate in a double boiler and add the coffee. When it is cool add 1 teaspoon of vanilla.

Whip the cream, and fold it into the chocolate mixture. Turn into the meringue shell and chill for two hours.

Note: If you do not own a double boiler then place the mixing bowl over a pan of hot water.

Drinks

Here are a few cocktails for those celebration days – or even for when you might just need cheering up!

J.T's Infamous Bloody Mary

This is sufficient for one drink!

60ml/2fl oz vodka
80ml/3fl oz tomato juice
15ml/1/2fl oz lemon juice
8 drops of Worcester sauce
3 drops of Tabasco sauce
1 teaspoon tomato ketchup
Freshly ground black pepper
A generous dash of celery salt

Combine all the ingredients in a jug and stir gently. Serve with ice to taste and garnish with lemon or a piece of celery – or both.

Pina Colada

I have included a recipe for Pina Colada as a trip to the Caribbean would not be complete without this delicious drink. I am also including a few other recipes for rum-based drinks for when you arrive in the Caribbean.

Serves two

120ml/4fl oz white rum
240ml/8fl oz pineapple juice
240ml/8fl oz coconut cream (unsweetened)
Crushed ice

Put all the ingredients into a blender and blend for about one minute. Serve in ice chilled glasses if possible.

Banana Daiquiri

I am also including a recipe for a Banana Daiquiri. A wonderful excuse for using up the glut of bananas that one inevitably has when crossing the Atlantic.

Serves two

120ml/4fl oz white rum
2 tablespoons of caster sugar
2 tablespoons of lemon juice
2 bananas, cut into pieces
Dash of Angostura Bitters (to taste)
12 ice cubes

Put all the ingredients into a blender and blend until all the ingredients are combined. Serve immediately.

Planter's Punch

Serves two

120ml/4fl oz dark rum
240ml/8fl oz orange juice
Juice of one lime
60ml/2fl oz grenadine
2 cups of crushed ice
Sugar to taste

Mix the above ingredients, except the crushed ice. Put the ice into glasses and pour the mixture over the ice. Serve.